T0302031

Managing As Mission

Managing As Mission: Nonprofit Managing for Sustainable Change

By
Lori Heninger, PhD

CRC Press
Taylor & Francis Group
Boca Raton London New York

CRC Press is an imprint of the
Taylor & Francis Group, an **informa** business
A CHAPMAN & HALL BOOK

CRC Press
Taylor & Francis Group
6000 Broken Sound Parkway NW, Suite 300
Boca Raton, FL 33487-2742

First issued in paperback 2021

© 2018 by Lori Heninger
CRC Press is an imprint of Taylor & Francis Group, an Informa business

No claim to original U.S. Government works

ISBN-13: 978-1-03-209653-7 (pbk)
ISBN-13: 978-1-138-74539-1 (hbk)

Library of Congress Cataloging-in-Publication Data

Names: Heninger, Lori, author.
Title: Managing as mission : nonprofit managing for sustainable change / Lori Heninger.
Description: Boca Raton, FL : CRC Press, [2017] | Includes bibliographical references.
Identifiers: LCCN 2017006895| ISBN 9781138745391 | ISBN 9781315180656 (ebook)
Subjects: LCSH: Nonprofit organizations--Management. | Leadership.
Classification: LCC HD62.6 .H455 2017 | DDC 658/.048--dc23
LC record available at https://lccn.loc.gov/2017006895

Visit the Taylor & Francis Web site at
http://www.taylorandfrancis.com

and the CRC Press Web site at
http://www.crcpress.com

Dedication

This book is dedicated to my husband, who
encouraged me to quit my day job

and

to all those managing to make the world a better place.

Contents

Preface

Just over a year ago, I was standing on the New Jersey Transit platform, waiting for the train to New York to take me to my job as Office Director and United Nations Representative for a large international non-governmental organization (or INGO, because around the UN everything is reduced to acronyms; there's no time to actually say things in their entirety given the pace of world events), for the last time. Five weeks before, I gave notice because I could no longer manage my office due to problems within the organization, problems whose results trickled down to me. For the first time in my adult life, I quit one job without having another lined up.

I was not having an "Eat, Pray, Love" moment, although my ability to resign was because my husband, Marc, works full time, my daughter is grown, and we have some savings. But as I write, she is getting married, and Marc and I are paying for much of the wedding. We have a mortgage, student loans, and Molly, a 90-pound Labrador (the title of her book is "Eat, Eat, Love"). So although this was in most ways a first-world problem, there were consequences to my actions. Quitting was more of a "Leap" (Vigeland, 2015) moment; a step off the edge of the career ledge without much of a net.

The worst part of quitting was that I felt that I was letting myself down. That somehow I had failed. I had accepted a job and, with over 20 years of national and international management experience, I could not make it work. I saw the problems with the organizational system as well as with the deficits in management, and after multiple tries and a year and a half of oral and written entreaties, became absolutely certain that things were not going to change. The organizational systems had become deeply focused on who was in charge—of program, messaging, and fundraising (money). Lines of communication and roles were unclear, decision-making was arbitrary, supervision did not exist, no one was listening to anyone other than those with whom they agreed—and the parameters for agreement stemmed from and were dictated by the leadership and those around the leadership. It was nonprofit work turned upside-down, the organization had become the point of focus instead of those the organization was created to help.

Marc urged me to leave for months prior to my actual resignation, but in keeping with my (stubborn) personality, I kept hoping things could get better. At one point he said to me, "Lori, you go to work every day and every day you get your heart broken." And it was true. I love my work. Love it. I don't want to die at my desk, but I need to work, to feel that I am contributing, being productive. I love to see and be part of individual and/or collective growth and change, of making the world even just a little better.

My heart was broken every time I tried without success to do something to make the structure and the management refocus on the mission, but that was almost impossible because the mission was unclear. In reality, one part of the organization was working to meet the existing mission, and the other part had decided to focus on a specific aspect of the mission, and there was no way the two groups were going to work together. The organization was in fiscal trouble, and fundraising was undertaken in areas that would have been considered "mission creep." My small staff was managed by individuals in another office. None of us was consulted regarding the organization's advocacy positions, which is the foundation of the policy work we were carrying out. Essentially, I was being paid to not work—not to supervise, not to think creatively, not to plan strategically. I played a lot of Spider Solitaire until I could no longer justify it to myself. I was hurt, I was frustrated, I was isolated; I had moved past anger to powerlessness, which is a place no one should ever be. Other staff in the organization at my level were frustrated and angry and hurt because we had no faith or trust in the people above us, and I know my staff were also frustrated and angry and hurt and, rightly, had little faith in me because I had checked out. And as much as I wanted to blame the organizational structure for the problems, my experience has shown me that in many ways it's less about structure, it's about organizational processes: the individuals, the relationships; about how we do things, as much as the mission, the outcome, the what we do.

I decided I would no longer be part of a system that hurt people, particularly in an organization that existed to help. So I quit.

* * *

For far too long, people have been blaming organizational structures in both the for-profit and the not-for-profit worlds for problems that may not actually be the fault of the structure. A traditional organizational chart is not necessarily bad, and a flat hierarchy is not necessarily the best solution. It's much easier to tweak the structure than to look at how we as individuals and teams do things, our motivations, our beliefs, our values, our fears; it's much more difficult to change our thinking and actions in ways that reflect the change we want to see in the world.

Instead of thinking about changing structure, maybe we should be asking how we achieve organization-wide clarity in mission, roles, policies, communication. Coupled with openness, approachability, responsibility, diversity, reflection, and a genuine interest in all stakeholders. And, as much as possible, an absence of fear. No surprises—I hate surprises relating to work. When roles, policies, and so on are clear, and when leadership is genuinely committed to creating a culture of inclusion and contribution, and is willing to embrace the struggles that go along with this, fear and uncertainty are reduced and people can get on with the work ... in ways that can create new opportunities and innovative ways forward.

During my life at work, I've struggled to form an area of "expertise" in my jobs; it seemed that this was the critical component to a successful career, technical knowledge of a subject area and relationships with the people working in that area: researchers, practitioners, organizational leaders, and, in the case of nonprofits, the funders who provide the fiscal resources to hire staff, provide program funds, keep a roof over our heads, pay for our airfares, and keep the copiers running. I've worked for or run organizations or networks focused on adolescent health, education in war and natural disaster, child soldiers, financing for development, mental health, homelessness, and more. I'm genuinely interested in all of it, but the "passion" that I was expecting for a specific thematic area of work always eluded me—why couldn't I just stick with one subject area? Why not just drill down and become an expert in that area? I have a PhD, there's no reason why I couldn't do it. It has seemed like a personal failure, like I didn't fit in with the way the nonprofit world is set up.

Over the past years, I've given this a lot of thought, and what I realized is that I am much more interested in the process of getting to ideas for change than in knowing about a specific subject area that may have prescriptions for change. I love being part of, or facilitating, discussions where ideas and possibilities are debated, and helping to direct that thinking based on what I am hearing. Of course it helps to know about the subject being discussed—in fact it's critically important. But the experience of "holding the space" so that people can arrive at new ways of approaching a problem is what really excites me. Working in partnership with those served expands my thinking. Supervising staff by asking questions instead of dictating solutions moves me. Getting in and figuring out what could work better, in conjunction with others, makes me want to come to work. Acknowledging that I, myself alone, don't know the best answer, living on the edge of ambiguity, harnessing the energy produced when people join in with what they know and listen to what others know, moving away from the fear of being wrong, of not having to have your idea rise to the top, of looking foolish, of going out on a limb with the possibility of losing your position as expert, is what thrills me. It's kind of like tightrope walking without a net but requires a lot less physical balance—which is good, because Philippe Petit I am not.

The process of acknowledging that "I know and don't know," that we all have knowledge and experience and at the same time holding that at bay to hear what others know and have experienced, can take us to a place of commonality, and knowing this may help to lessen the fear associated with the vulnerability it takes to get to that place of commonality. In the end, it's far less scary to know what others are thinking than to have to be on your guard and always guessing. If I know, then I can act.

I am by no means denigrating technical expertise or leadership. If my daughter needed surgery, I want someone with the best possible technical knowledge, the skill to operate, and all the tools and implements, equipment, and a sterile environment for the best possible outcome. I want aeronautical engineers designing airplanes—although no one asked me about leg room, and at 5'9" tall, economy class is tortuous—expert mechanics maintaining them, and experienced pilots in the cockpit. My concern is that, given that technical knowledge and experience is seen as most crucial, the processes that can lead to real change can be denigrated as something that is not helpful to reaching a solution and making progress. If an expert already knows, what's the point of discussion? Start with the expert and create a program. Including everyone—and I mean everyone, staff, those served, and so on—just takes too long. In the nonprofit world, there's no money for it. Just implement the expert's solution. Build institutions that ensure the technical people are at the top, and the rest of the structure is just the means to getting things done. The "hands-on/technical work" is the real work; your credibility comes from that, whether it is humanitarian work in a war zone or preventing child marriage.

If technical knowledge is placed above all, if there are those who know and others who need to learn (or, more cynically, those who don't know and need to be told), if managing and the process involved always seem less important, it follows that organizational systems exist only to support the technical work. The idea of managing as a vehicle to the organizational vision and mission is an afterthought—or no thought at all. If organizational structures, systems, and management including meetings, hiring, and supervising staff, fundraising, budgets, and so on are seen as components needed to support technical expertise, then everything is constructed with expertise sitting at the top. If the goal is getting things done/made/fixed, and technical people are in charge and know how to do/make/fix, there is an inherent power hierarchy in organizational structure and systems, and a potential separation between people based on that power differential.

And while this may be fine for building airplanes—although my knees disagree—we in nonprofits need to ask ourselves if this is really the best way to go about structuring our work and our organizations. In the nonprofit world, we are working with people, environments, cultures, not building the same plane/car/computer over and over. If we have organized ourselves to crank out "cures"—which have been amazing for preventing illnesses because most people's physiology responds similarly—we are treating everyone the same, and we know that this is not optimal in the highly complex situations in which nonprofits often work. If we are relying mainly on technical solutions to solve our problems and meet our needs, and we are not considering how we make decisions on what should be done, how they are implemented, and by whom, then we are locked into structures, ways of organizing the world, that do not honor the complexity and humanity in the people with whom we and our organizations work, those on our staffs/teams, or ourselves. We are shortchanging everyone through a mechanistic way of looking at and undertaking our work. We are constrained by time, money, and fear, and while time and money are part of the fabric of life of a nonprofit, fear should not be.

We in the nonprofit world need more balance between the technical of applied interventions—although we need to have respect for and include scientific data and experience—and the process of posing a problem/challenge, discussing the needs and fears underlying the challenge, then moving to a solution that comes from people contributing what they know into the mix. When this occurs, learning happens. Relationships are built. Ownership emerges. People grow. Sustainable solutions that can lead to further change are implemented. Organizations want sustainability. Donors want sustainability. Everyone wants sustainability. Technical expertise without inclusive processes is unsustainable. This is true both in the work that is done outside the organization and the work that is done inside the organization. To use an overused phrase, we have to be the change we want to see.

My goal in writing this book is to ask the nonprofit world to look at itself: its leadership, operations, and structures, and principally its management, through a lens pointed toward a changed concept of mission. The "how" of getting to the organization's mission/goal must become as important as the goal itself. The relationships, whether to another person, to a job, to a mission, are often discounted in our race to get the job done and, in fact, relationships are at the root of reaching organizational missions, and of a changed world. Form must follow function; and while we can talk ad infinitum about organizational structures—and they are important—it is in the act of managing that the "how," the internal processes that mirror the path to the external change, are realized and can create sustainability. We need to know our strengths and weaknesses, have an agreed-upon understanding of the mission, a clear direction, and balance between the technical and the process. I'm hoping that the information herein can be like the tightrope walker's pole, increasing the possibility of staying the course to the other side.

Are these ideas naïve? Perhaps. Am I hopeful that we can change the world—and ourselves—through managing? Always. Is there experience that it can work? Yes.

Acknowledgments

This book would not have been written in its present form without title guidance from Irwin Epstein, who has pulled me through large writing projects on more than one occasion. Thank you, Irwin. Readers of early drafts—to whom I am deeply grateful—are Chloe Frielen-Olewitz, Thea Heninger-Lowell, Nazima Kadir, Steve Ross, Michael Snarr, and Kerstin Tebbe. Gay Edelman read, commented on, and edited the proposal, steering my writing back to the ocean after I had gone too far down a small river. Thank you. To Subhadra Belbase, Heyon-Ju Rho, Holly Fancher, Matt Michels, Sarah Stevenson, and Terri Blair, thank you for your generosity of spirit and inputs. To my memorable managers, Julie Lorenzo and Joe DiGenova at the Center for Urban Community Services, thank you for your examples as managers/leaders and your commitment to housing for all. Thank you to team members in many organizations who taught me how to manage as mission—you have made this book possible and have made my life better by knowing and working with you.

A special thank you to my husband Marc Engle, who believed in this book and in me, and provided all the support and tea I could ever have needed while writing it. Marc also provided cover design and all original artwork. This book would not exist without you.

Chapter 1

Why Managing
As Mission?

1.1 Why Managing As Mission?

Hi! I'm glad you are here.

If you were really here, in person, I'd ask you if you wanted tea or coffee or water (or if it were later I'd offer you a *drink* drink), and we'd have a face-to-face chat, and we could actually talk about our ideas about managing as mission. But since I'm writing and you are reading, you are going to have to make your own beverage, and hopefully the sentences and chapters that follow will allow a conversation to start in your head—and your heart. And doubly hopefully, you'll take those thoughts and talk about them with others with whom you work.

Managing As Mission: Nonprofit Managing for Sustainable Change has been written for nonprofit managers, leaders, boards, and people who may someday be in one or more of these positions. Its core premise is to demonstrate that by linking the following three things—the organizational mission (why the organization exists and what it is supposed to do); the process by which we get to the mission; and the way we manage our staffs and ourselves—we can create systems, interactions, and ways of thinking *within* our organizations, which are models for the world we want to see *outside* the organization.

Managing As Mission will allow you and those in (and outside) your nonprofit organization to

- Reframe the idea of nonprofit mission by considering the origin of "mission."
- Gain an agreed-upon, values- and relationship-based understanding of how your organization will achieve its reoriented mission.
- Embrace managing as a method for promoting and utilizing that understanding.
- Increase credibility with those served by the organization and others in the nonprofit world.

As both a book and an idea, *Managing As Mission* bridges the publishing categories of Management and Self-Help; if we are going to see a different and better world, both people *and* processes need to change: It's not just one or the other. Relationships are central to that change, and this book will give you information and exercises on working relationships—the kind in which managers, staffs, and systems are impacted and changed by working together to reach the mission, and which result in an organization that is reflective of a better world.

Now that you have an idea of where we are going, let's start with an example of managing described by a friend of mine:

A few years ago, I was hired to run a [X] program at a large advocacy organization. The organization's mission was to ensure women's health, age 18+, internationally, focusing on things like the International Day of Action for Women's Health, the UN's Commission on the Status of Women, partnering with groups like the International Women's Health Coalition, Planned Parenthood International, and others on campaigns to change policy. I came into the organization really excited and with high hopes, I had heard it "walked the walk" and was deeply mission-driven. I had a small team based in the same office and I was told that essentially, I could run my team as I saw fit within the mission and strategic plan of the organization. My boss told me that he was really committed to getting inputs and opinions and I was excited to bring my experience to the new job. I had a lot of first-hand experience in both the U.S. and in humanitarian situations as a health educator and was glad to be able to use it for advocacy work.

During orientation, I got my first red flag; in a meeting with my boss and the managers that made up his team, I watched him ask questions and then tell each person—in a very nice way—why their idea would not work, how they needed to change their thinking, sometimes pulling one idea out of what they said and dismissing the others. It was clear that he had something in his head that he wanted, and was asking questions to try to steer all of us toward his goal, his thinking. I really thought it was odd because he was talking about building wells and advocating for potable water for boys and girls, and it was clear that the organization's mission was to advocate for women's health. At the end of that discussion, he mentioned that there was a grant available to work with [a coalition of humanitarian organizations] on issues of children and water, and that this would be a great opportunity for the organization. After the meeting, I asked someone—it was uncomfortable because I didn't know anyone yet—and she looked at me and rolled her eyes before she said, "What can you do?" and walked away. She did say hi and introduced herself and I introduced myself but that was it.

Later, after eating lunch alone—I thought there might be a plan for me to meet people, especially those who were at the same level as me so I could get to know them—I met with my boss. It was obvious he was really, really smart, and that he had some experience, but definitely not as much hands-on as me. So I sat down and the first thing he said after a couple minutes of talking was something like, "Wow, can you believe that meeting this morning? I was trying to get a point across and all I got was resistance. I've been working on this grant for months and I just can't get people to come around. I just don't get it. It's a lot of money, it's raising our profile."

I was, I want to say surprised, but really I was shocked. So I asked him what he thought the problem was and he went on and on about [a colleague] saying that she was stubborn, not a team player, and she was openly contradicting him and she was impeding progress. He also said that nobody liked her, that she kept her team separate from the rest of the managers' teams. I did not know what to say, anything that I said could be taken the wrong way and I didn't want to start off in a bad way, on a bad foot. So I sat there and listened to him for 10 minutes talk about all the issues he has and how he wants to move things forward but there's a lot of resistance except from the CEO who thinks the same way he does about grants and expansion and how we get the organization's name out there. He told me about the great relationship they have, how she goes to him when she has questions, you get it. I tried to bring things back to my work with some success, we talked about what he expected from me—never asked me what I expected from him—gave me a bunch of stuff to read like the strategic plan dashboard, job descriptions, marking and branding guidelines and more and told me that we'd have a call in a couple of days. The office where he worked and where I worked were in two different places. When I was leaving his office, he asked me to straighten out a picture that was hanging on his wall, which I did and now I feel sick just saying that.

A week went by and I didn't hear anything, but my staff were in regular touch with him. I did a lot of things in the office, set up my systems, got to know my staff, we had a lunch together, I set up meeting schedules and found out what they were doing. I still didn't hear from my boss and I finally sent a meeting request during the middle of the next week and got a bounce back that he was traveling. I had no idea. My staff knew, but I didn't. Really?? He'd talk with them, email them about stuff—work, I think some of it was personal. But I couldn't get him to set up a meeting with me. Then finally he sent a meeting request for a 30-minute meeting the next week and then canceled it 15 minutes before we were supposed to talk. He said that it was an "emergency finance meeting." I had an agenda, I had a lot of questions, and then I had no one to ask. The other managers and I hadn't had a team meeting with him since that first one, and I had no idea when we'd have another, and I wasn't in an office with anyone else at my level, so I didn't have a relationship with them and I didn't know what to do. My staff were nice to me, there wasn't any overt friction, in our meetings when I asked them about program work, or whatever, they'd tell me what they were doing and for the most part it was aligning with the mission and advocacy. They were both really passionate about women's health and it was great that at least in that way we were all on the same page. I set up weekly staff meetings for my team.

I decided to email the people from the team meeting just to see if I could start to get to know them, you know, what they do, ideas for my area, what had been done, how they thought about the work. Three out of four wrote back, and the one that didn't had an out of office message, she was on vacation. I set up calls for that week and for the most part they were really helpful. I finally felt like I knew something about the strategy—you know, you can read the documents but how they get translated into action can be different. Anyway they told me a lot, even the one who rolled her eyes—she really wanted to talk and not just about the work. I was really leery about getting into this with her so kept directing back to the work. The one who he said was stubborn talked the least and really pushed on the mission and how we needed to stick to it in the work. Then she said, "But maybe you shouldn't be talking to me given I'm not so popular with [the boss]." Again, I wanted to keep the call about work, and I thanked her for talking to me, and we hung up.

Early the next week, I get a call from [boss] who told me that he heard I had talked with the team and it was pretty clear that he was edgy. I said I had, and that it was really helpful to me to get to know them, their take on the work. And then he got mad. Saying things like, "You need to come to me first, you need to be getting your information from me, I talk to everyone and if you have questions text me, I get 500 emails a day and I can't get through them all, I'm totally overworked" and on and on and on. I was totally, utterly shocked. I felt like I had done something wrong—like talking to my colleagues is wrong—at least it wasn't in my last job—and that he was the only one I should get information from. Or talk to. After some more dressing down, he stopped, and I was silent, I had no idea what to say. I needed the job and I really didn't know him and I didn't know what to do. So like all "good girls," I apologized. *APOLOGIZED! IN A WOMEN'S ORGANIZATION!* I thought I was going to be living the dream, but it was turning into a fucking nightmare. He talked some more, told me why it was important to go through him again, and after a little while he said, "Don't worry, my bark is worse than my bite." And at that point, I knew this was probably not going to work. I was furious. Not just angry, livid. I'd stick it out as long as I could but I knew I'd probably have to look for another job.

One problem was that I was alone. I was isolated with no one to talk to. I had no real authority over my own staff—and that wasn't even what I was looking for, I just wanted to have some way of doing what I was hired to do—manage the office and work on women's health. I eventually went to human resources but it took forever for them to get back to me and I got more pissed. I thought about talking to his boss, the CEO, but I'd seen their interactions in meetings and knew, because everything had to go through him, that that would be disaster. I had some off-line chats with other managers and started to get to know them a little, but it was clear that everyone was pretty much in the same situation and that things had been tried to make change but nothing changed. They told me that in the main office, people spent more time complaining about people, him included, than doing the work.

I started to feel invisible. It was clear to me that I wasn't needed, my staff were ok doing work given to them by my boss. Nobody asked me anything, nobody needed anything from me, ideas I had were either shot down or ignored, it was like I didn't exist. I was totally demoralized. And as much as I hate to say this, I used my time at work to look for another job. And I found one in another organization that focuses on research and advocacy with girls and women. It's not perfect but it's a whole hell of a lot better than what I was dealing with. I'm much happier, I'm actually doing work, good work, with my team and we are seeing policy change and that's completely exciting. Communication is good up, down and across lines and it's really helpful. Lots of group decision-making. I get a lot of ideas from people and they say they get good ideas from me. My direct service experience is really helpful.

I never want to be in a situation like that other one again. I really got how it feels to be ignored, to feel like what you have to say or to offer isn't asked for, isn't wanted. And abused. Probably like a lot of the women we work with and for feel. So that was my worst experience in being managed and my goal is to make sure I don't ever do that to my staff. It was unbelievable.*

* * *

Sorry to start our chat with such a negative story. I'm wondering if you can see yourself being managed, your experience, in any part of this situation. Or if you are a manager, whether you have made some of these mistakes. Take a minute to identify the specific things that impacted you. You might even jot them down if that would be helpful.

The nonprofit described in the previous passage is an example of a nonprofit organization managed, at least in the division described, in a way that is secretive, segmented,

---

* This story is a compilation of stories told to me by people interviewed for this book. It is not linked to any one organization or person.

siloed, competitive, hierarchical, isolating, diminishing, abusive, off-mission, self-involved, and self-interested; not reflective of a world in which people are equal, valued, heard, lifted, lifting, collaborative, open, flourishing, focused. The structure, management, processes, and behaviors do not seem to reflect a world in which people's voices, especially those of women, are lifted up and respected. Mental health does not seem to be valued, and attempts at internal advocacy fell on plugged ears. In fact, women were actively, if unconsciously, demeaned. It is an illustration that, even though this organization may be in some ways meeting its mission, the way it is getting to the mission—the internal methodologies linked to how the organization is managed—is deeply flawed, causing staff to feel angry, frustrated, invisible, and unhappy. And as much as we might want to build a barrier between our emotions and our work, some of these feelings are going to spill over, either at work or in our personal lives.

Research in the for-profit sector has shown that staff who are frustrated and unhappy are less productive and lack the desire to innovate (Oswald et al., 2014) and are the main reasons good staff leave—according to Victor Lipman's (2015b) *The Type B Manager: Leading Successfully in a Type A World*, people leave managers, not companies. In 2013, the head of the Gallup organization wrote "Here's something they'll probably never teach you in business school." Gallup CEO Jim Clifton observed, "The single biggest decision you make in your job—bigger than all the rest—is who you name manager. When you name the wrong person manager, nothing fixes that bad decision. Not compensation, not benefits—nothing."

This is coming from the for-profit sector. Which leads me to ask, why would those of us in the nonprofit world—people of passion, commitment to eliminating poverty and violence against children, providing healthcare, protecting endangered species and habitat, working to mitigate climate change—knowing that good managing, inclusion, and relationship-building are keys to success, create organizational systems and engage in ways of managing that perpetuate all that we are working to change? Why would we manage our staff in a way that undermines that process? The very idea of it makes me so sad.

* * *

I love the nonprofit world. And I am very frustrated by it. I have spent most of my professional life in the nonprofit sector, and much of that in international development, humanitarian response, and policy creation, in both large and small organizations, in the U.S. and in other countries. I have found similarities and differences between myself and almost every person I have ever met, whether working in refugee camps in Chad, with youth in Northern Uganda, in a women's shelter in New York, or with diplomats at the United Nations. More importantly, I've learned something from almost everyone I've met, and I have been changed by meeting them, by listening to them. By testing ideas with them. By the relationships that have developed that pushed me to think differently about how I see the world. By being told that maybe the way I saw something wasn't the way another person saw it. In each organization I was working toward the achievement of a mission, but the process of getting to the mission, and how the organization was managed, was wildly different from one to the next. In some it was helpful. In others, not so much.

If we want to see change in the world, inclusive, sustainable change, we in nonprofits have to demonstrate that we are not expecting others to do what we have not been able to do ourselves: change. And that change needs to be based on the world we want.

Throughout the book I will refer to "the world we want" or "the world we want to see." My frame of reference for this world is based on the United Nations Charter, the Universal Declaration of Human Rights, and the Sustainable Development Goals: a world without violent conflict; that acknowledges and lifts up the inherent dignity and worth of the human being; establishes the equality of men and women (and if you include the Convention on the Rights of the Child, children too); provides justice for all through the rule of law; allows for and encourages social progress, inclusion and a celebration of diversity, freedom of speech and belief and from fear and want, an equitable standard of living, climate action, and responsible production and consumption. If this is not the world you want to see, it's good you found out now so that you can read something else. If it is, and if you are or might become a nonprofit manager, we can through our actions undertake to create a world within our organizations that reflects the world we want to see outside our organizations, moving us at least one step closer to creating that world.

In addition to envisioning the world we want, we have to be as clear about how to get there as we are about where we are going. If we are committed to, for example, sustainable community development, implicit in that is the idea that we should work to put ourselves out of business by lessening or eliminating the reasons for our being—solving problems in collaboration with those experiencing the problems—creating equitable, participatory processes for long-term problem-solving, and then stepping out of the way. Does everyone in the organization agree that this is the goal? Has anyone ever asked the question? What about the people in the community, have they been asked? Has there been a discussion about the idea and what it would mean for how the organization works, both externally and internally? By asking the question, engaging in discussion and reaching a decision, a means–ends process has begun.

Linking means and ends will have an impact on how organizations interpret their structures. My experience and my theoretical foundation have oriented me to the idea that the nonprofit organizational mission and those being served were at the top of the organizational chart, and everything else flowed from that. Location, board, structure, staffing, systems, everything. While I still believe that the mission has to be the point from which everything else in the nonprofit flows, mission needs to be as much process-driven as goal-driven. Reaching the mission has to be inclusive, people need to be heard and acknowledged, and they need to be treated equitably. It's good to recognize that we don't and can't know it all—it can actually take a lot of the pressure off.

Linking means and ends, seeing the relationship between them, also implies a process of getting to a mission and as a reflection of the mission itself, and leads to taking a different view of "management." It necessitates moving from "management," a static idea, a noun, an idea, to "managing," a process, a verb. Linking ends and means moves us to make a choice, to decide to manage our organizations in ways that reflect the change we want to see, because *how* we get to mission is as important as, or more important than, *mission accomplished*. The process is the product is the process. *Managing As Mission* provides a way to unite means and ends through managing.

During an interview for this book, the leader of an international nonprofit said,

> I think a lot of times people become very mission-oriented, and that can become equated with if you achieve the results, the means don't matter. I happen to believe, think that's wrong. Means do matter. The mission is about having conversations, and recognizing that everyone has something to contribute, and getting people to talk about it. To come together and work together to build something greater than any individual can. If we don't operate ourselves that way, it's not only hypocritical, [it's] also very counterproductive. Any results we do achieve, anything we do accomplish, is weaker because we didn't do it in the right way, because we didn't live up to its ideals. So I think that whether it's trying to attract donors,

or trying to link with partners, it's that you're okay with it because it's what you have to do to try to get to the next step. You have to take the time to work through that. You don't want to just be about "mission accomplished." How you do it is about how it grows and about sustainability.

Part of this way of working, of managing, is external to you as an individual: having the tools and structures to ensure good planning and strategy, fiscal management and oversight, legal compliance, organizational charts, and so on. Part of this is internal: being willing to listen and to be changed by what one is hearing. Being able to hold two (or three or four) different ideas and work to discern how to move forward. Honoring what you know, your experience, being willing to acknowledge that others honor what *they* know and *their* experience, and to struggle together to come to a new way of knowing, a new experience, a new way forward. Dialogue, transparency, and responsibility create the atmosphere where staff and those the organization is designed to serve can flourish. And sometimes fail, because none of us runs at 100-percent success. As a manager, it's how you respond to success and failure, internally and externally, that makes the difference.

If we want to change the way the world looks, if we want to ensure greater equality, we may have to reimagine vision and mission within the context of the process—the *means* part of means and ends, the *how* we get to the goal—and then determine what managing looks like when mission and process are rolled together. Do we want a process, a way of getting to the mission, that replicates the status quo? Or do we want a process in which change includes everyone—even *us*? Where the lines between helper and helped are diminished? Where people can solve their own problems—because problems are never going to stop, and at some point our organizations will close their doors, or we will retire, or pass from this world, and either someone will take over or the work will end. So why not create a system where you work to turn the problem-solving over to someone else? Include others in decision-making? Listen full-on? Really, it's in your best interest. Think of all the things you could do if you didn't have to work the incredible long hours you put into your current job. Maybe a nice massage?

In the chapters following, I will describe the origins and history of the idea of "mission," and why we need to reconsider the idea and function of mission in light of this history. Next, we'll take a look at the ideas behind the process of getting to the mission, and how the means can become the ends and vice versa. Then we'll consider managing, what it means, the systems, structures, and actions that make up the job, and the importance of relationships. After that we'll tie it all together, mission, managing, and process, with some thought exercises and a couple of tools that might be helpful to you in your work. Last, we'll look at ways forward.

* * *

Some of the terminology in *Managing As Mission* is a product of our acronym-crazy world, and I have tried to use full organizational names/titles as much as possible. When referring to the for-profit sector, I use "for-profit," "corporation," or "company" synonymously, and do the same with the terms "nonprofit" and "organization." For the purpose of this book, nonprofits include organizations that would be categorized as a U.S.-based 501(c)3, or an organization anywhere that does not have shareholders and is working toward a goal that is not profit-based.

While envisioning this book, I became acutely aware of two dilemmas. The first is whether the ideas presented are universal, or whether they reflect a northern/western orientation to managing, organizations, and a better world. The second is that "a better world," as defined by me, may not be the "better world" defined by all nonprofit groups or individuals in those groups. Regarding the first dilemma, the fact is that I am from the United States and have mainly managed staff and organizations based in the U.S., albeit with an international reach. I have managed staff in other countries, and some of my most profound learnings on how to get to a mission have come from my work in other countries; these have become ingrained in the way I work and manage, and it has become more and more difficult to tease them out over time. Knowing this, my hope is that you, the reader, will take what is useful to you and your context and forgive or let me know about my blind spots and any overreaching.

As for the second dilemma, my hope is that we can at least agree on the worth and dignity of each human being, as well as their internationally agreed-upon human rights as a starting point.

This book has been developed through multiple sources: structured interviews; stories told by nonprofit workers and people whom nonprofits have served; academic literature; blogs; and my own experiences. My hope is that by utilizing managing as a process to achieving the organizational mission, the means can become the ends on a day-to-day basis. From this genuine change on a small scale a better world, that works better for all, can be created.

So refill your cup, and let's go.

Chapter II

The Mission

This chapter is going to drill down into nonprofit mission statements; first, we'll have a look at why nonprofits have missions, and consider the differences between for-profit and nonprofit mission statements. After that, we'll think about the etymology of "mission" and how its origins are impacting the way in which nonprofits do their work.

Nonprofits have created vision and mission statements for three reasons:

- First, so that people both inside and outside the organization know why they exist. *Save the Children* is pretty clear even without vision and mission statements; *Acumen* (Acumen, 2016), an organization whose tag line is "changing the way the world tackles poverty," maybe not so much without the tag line.
- Second, to provide benchmarks to determine whether the organization has been successful in its work.
- Third, to help with decision-making, avoiding "mission creep" (Top Nonprofits, 2016).

The vision of an organization is traditionally the big "what," the ultimate goal that you want to see achieved, even if you may not see it in your lifetime. An end to cancer. A world free of violence and injustice. Clean oceans. It's the world one wants.

The world "one" wants (ok, the world *I* want…) has been described in Chapter I. I'm probably not going to get to see many of those goals being fully realized in my lifetime, given I was born in the last millennium, but I want my daughter and, if she has children, I want my grandchildren to live in a world where those goals are enacted and are the norm. I want you and your children to have them. And your grand-children, and so on. The whole orientation of this book is to work for (and hopefully achieve) sustainable, fear-reducing, ongoing social and environmental change through manag-ing. Lifting people up. Working together, cooperation. It does not leave a lot of room for exclusion or hate, or for open carry in the workplace. Yes, National Rifle Association (NRA) Foundation, I am talking to you. Still, if the NRA Foundation wants to buy and read the book and utilize the ideas, I'm all for it! Please feel free. Actually, I'll send you a free copy. Signed. But you can't use it for target practice—for that you'll have to fork over the greenbacks.

2.1 One Vision, Three Missions

Organizations develop mission statements for the three rea-sons in the opening paragraphs: identification, measuring, and guidance. Mission helps us to tell one organization from another.

Potable water is one of the most pressing issues interna-tionally. Some 633 million people do not have access to clean drinking water, and this is not solely an issue for developing countries, as Americans in Flint, Michigan and other U.S. cities know too well. There are a significant number of organiza-tions focused on ensuring potable water for all (the vision), but how an organization has decided to reach the vision—as delineated by the ideas contained in the mission statement—is different for different organizations. The mission of the Thirst Project is "by educating and reaching out to students, the Thirst Project aims to educate and motivate young people to dissolve the global water crisis" (2016). Splash's mission is "an organization that works with foreign governments and builds local businesses to create scalable, sustainable safe water projects in vulnerable cities" (2016). Blood:Water's is "a nonprofit that partners with African grassroots organizations to bring clean water and HIV/AIDS support to 1 million people in 11 countries" (Chung, 2015).

Three nonprofit organizations, three different ways to get to potable water. One focuses on educating students, which would imply curriculum development and advocacy training, and delineates work with a specific group determined to be change-makers. Another partners with governments to develop scalable, private sector projects, and describes its work as focusing on urban areas. The last one partners with grassroots organizations and focuses on a specific population, people with HIV/AIDS, in a specific geographic region, Africa.

One vision, three clear and different ways of getting there. Each contains variables that can be operationalized for measurement. Splash can count the number of scalable private sector projects it has created; however, it probably will not be able to count the projects it doesn't know about because one of its goals is "Theft"—the organization *wants* people to steal the technology for potable water so that it spreads organically. The Thirst Project can measure the number of students with whom it works, and can determine the work done by students through the results of their fundraising efforts. The money is then used for clean water technology including wells, which can also be measured. Measurement in nonprofits is critical; we need to know if what we are doing works to ensure we are doing no harm, and that people or trees or endangered species are actually benefiting from our interventions. Oh, and we also need to be able to tell donors how we did.

Vision and mission statements can be seen as fixed and/or malleable. The vision is, in most cases, probably more fixed than the mission, just by its scope (big). The mission is also somewhat fixed; if Splash suddenly decided it was going to focus on ensuring that adolescent girls had access to potable water in rural areas with no rationale provided, eyebrows might be raised. The mission would have shifted significantly, questions would arise regarding the ability of the organization to deliver on the mission, level of internal expertise, contacts on the ground, funding. If Splash, in its work, had seen a recurrent need regarding adolescent girls and water, it might think about undertaking a needs assessment on what is still not being addressed regarding water needs, and this may lead to working on behalf of adolescent girls in rural areas. That could make sense if the expertise was available internally, and partner governments wanted to or could be convinced to take this on. Or, Splash may contact another organization that focuses on girls or works to provide community water sources, and let them know that they are seeing this as an unmet need.

Or perhaps, in Splash's work, there were unforeseen conse-quences of working with governments on urban water sup-plies, like a lack of skilled people to install and subsequently repair broken water lines. This might create a shift in mission, or the organization may partner with another organization who knows how to educate people to do plumbing. Both of these examples could create the need for a tweak or change in mission statement.

Vision and mission statements can be created in multiple ways. They can be developed by an individual, by the orga-nization's board, as part of a larger consultative process, or by a hired agency. Nonprofits have been started with a great idea from a person who was committed to making a change. Maybe the person was an expert in their field. Maybe they saw someone or something that needed help. Maybe they

were driven by their faith. Or maybe they lead a very successful for-profit and wanted to redistribute their wealth.* In other
organizations, the mission has been created in consultation
with staff and people who are recipients of services. One of
the people interviewed for this book provided an example:

> The mission statement has been created by a team
> within the organization, in consultation with a con-
> sultant who has a background in branding and
> communications. And it has been shared with our
> partners. As part of the strategy it went out for con-
> sultation, so children and young people have been
> asked to provide feedback on it, plus groups of indi-
> viduals coming together in various countries around
> the world.

Nonprofit organizations are nearly always competing for
funds, just as for-profits are competing for customers. Because
of this competition, nonprofits have enlisted the expertise of
advertising agencies to create mission statements and small-
and large-scale campaigns to increase funding. Ad agencies
can develop vision and mission statements, tag lines, logos,
regular communications with the public including inbound
marketing, websites, commercials, print ads, and donation
requests. In 2011, it was estimated, based on reviews of IRS
forms from 71 nonprofits with revenues of >USD10 million
per year, that USD7.6 billion was spent on advertising and
marketing (Watson, 2011). This means that unless there was a
specific process for inputs from a wide group, as delineated in
the previous quote, the creation of mission and vision is moving further away from those served and from those doing the
work, and is moving more toward for-profit branding.

---

* Or maybe someone is driven by guilt or anxiety. As head of a company, maybe
  they want publicity, or a tax deduction or to garner future customers. It's certainly not for me to judge, but I have seen all of the above.

2.2 For-Profit and Nonprofit Vision and Mission Statements: Similar and Different

Both for-profit companies and nonprofit organizations have vision and mission statements, and if we look first at the vision statement, we'll see that they play essentially the same role in both: a statement of the big picture. It is in the mission statement where the divergence between for-profits and nonprofits occurs, although both use the mission as a benchmark. The difference is that in for-profits, the benchmark is profit, and in nonprofits, the benchmark is a better world. Although to read many current for-profit mission statements, you might think otherwise. Here are a few examples:

■ Coca-Cola: To refresh the world—in mind, body and spirit ... To inspire moments of optimism—through our brands and actions ... To create value and make a difference everywhere we engage.
■ Nike: To bring inspiration and innovation to every athlete* in the world.
■ Levi's: People love our clothes and trust our company. We will market the most appealing and widely worn casual clothing in the world. We will clothe the world.
■ Starbucks: To inspire and nurture the human spirit—one person, one cup and one neighborhood at a time.

Next, some nonprofit mission statements:

■ Save the Children: To inspire breakthroughs in the way the world treats children and to achieve immediate and lasting change in their lives.
■ TED: Spreading ideas.
■ Oxfam: To create lasting solutions to poverty, hunger, and social injustice.

---

* Athlete means *everyone*.

- Amnesty International: To undertake research and action focused on preventing and ending grave abuses of human rights.
- Audubon: To conserve and restore natural ecosystems, focusing on birds, other wildlife, and their habitats for the benefit of humanity and the earth's biological diversity.
- Doctors Without Borders (Médecins Sans Frontières) works in nearly 70 countries, providing medical aid to those most in need regardless of their race, religion, or political affiliation.

Interesting, right? Mission statements from both for-profits and nonprofits use altruistic language. Love. Inspiration. Optimism. Conserve. Restore. Solutions. Although I have not been able to find a history of the change in the language of for-profit mission statements, I would venture to say that the move toward the inclusion of socially conscious language in these statements is not accidental, given that mission equates to profit, and to increase profits one needs to reach the widest possible group of stakeholders/customers. Altruistic, personalized language appeals to people. I would also say that nonprofit mission statements have gotten much crisper, with carefully selected words that can be translated into variables and measured, while still conveying the idea of the organization's purpose. The problem comes in when, through the mission, we are equating measuring change in the environment or people's lives with selling cans of Coke.

Companies measure their mission—profit—by profit and loss statements: either they meet costs and show profit or they don't. Systems and jobs are aligned to ensuring that the bottom line—profit—is met. The rest of it is nice language, "refreshing the world in mind body and spirit, to inspire moments of optimism through our brands and actions" is all good, but at the end of the day, if people who are sad are drinking Coke, and people who don't feel refreshed in their spirit by drinking Coke are still drinking Coke, I'm just not sure that Coke is going to branch out into the psychotherapy business. I'm not sure they care, as long as that person keeps buying Coke. I completely believe that the people at Coke would be glad if a by-product of purchasing and consuming their beverage made people happier, but it's not the bottom line.

For nonprofits, measuring is often a bit more uncertain, because calculating change in things like behavior or learning is more difficult than counting cans or dollars. Measuring the impact of programs and efforts, while not impossible, is hampered by staff fears about research, lack of funds to carry out research, and intervening variables.

When someone buys a Coke, the sale is recorded. It's clear that something has happened. Coke selected, money paid. There is a tally. It can be measured fairly easily. If the Coca-Cola company wants to know what triggered that person to buy their product, they set up a process to find out; they have determined that knowing why someone buys their product is helpful to their future sales. The private sector budgets for and invests in research and development, market research, and advertising, both before and after a product is released. They know it is in the best interest of their mission, the bottom line, to spend the money and know what people want.

Measuring impact in both for-profits and nonprofits is critically important; in for-profits, it is important to know the funds coming in to determine how to operate, expand, retool, hire, lay off, and so on. Oh, and to deliver dividends to shareholders. In nonprofits, it's critical for the same reasons (minus the shareholder part—nonprofits don't have shareholders, there is no fiscal return on investment, although you do get to feel satisfaction for a job well done) but, more importantly, so that we know what works, we are accountable to those we serve and those who fund us and again, most importantly, so that we do no harm. But in the nonprofit sector, measuring impact is still a bit of a dilemma for organizations. Part of it is the availability of tools, part is understanding research, and part is resources (money and time).

Regarding tools, social scientists have utilized both quantitative and qualitative methodologies, have worked diligently to define variables, and have realized innovative ways of measuring change. Dr. Irwin Epstein (2009) developed the process of Clinical Data Mining, a user-friendly, low-cost way of utilizing existing clinical data to build knowledge, impact clinical decision-making, and help clinical practitioners reflect on their work. At Massachusetts Institute of Technology (MIT), d-lab (Development through Discovery, Design, and Dissemination) has formed Lean Research, a framework and approach for development and humanitarian field research. Citizen-led research on children's learning has been a successful monitoring and measuring methodology, and results have shaped education policy (ACER, 2015).

Research can be a scary term. Even though I did my PhD on the ethics of research with unaccompanied children in conflict settings, I still feel uncertain when I think about setting up a measuring program/protocol for nonprofit work. I know I am not alone. People become paralyzed by this fear, and instead of measuring even something small, they just don't do it. People may think, "it's not really needed because 'we know we are doing a good job'." And it is time consuming, even with new methodologies; it is additional work to review charts, to integrate tracking systems, or to take a variable, break it down into its component parts, and then find a valid, reliable research instrument to measure what you want to measure. Never mind the actual implementation of the survey, data collection and analysis, and reporting results. As I said previously, many corporations build this in; it's in the budget and is shown as part of the monthly profit and loss statement (because they are measuring money).

Although nonprofit donors want empirical information on the outcomes of their giving, there has been a consistent lack of willingness to provide the funding to support rigorous processes, pushing this down onto nonprofits as an unfunded mandate. Because of a lack of resources, we are often left with "counting things," number of interventions given, people served, books provided, when what we would really like to do is to determine if what we have done has made change. We call this output (counting) versus outcome (impact/change). An interviewee commented on this, saying

> and it's hard to explain that because people want to know if you've done X number vaccinations, the number of books you've distributed. But it doesn't matter if the kids aren't actually going to school and using those books, and if they aren't learning.

Those of us in the nonprofit world want to know if what we are doing is helping, not solely because donors demand it, but because we want to know if those we are serving or working with are being positively impacted by our work. It's why we went into this work in the first place, the intrinsic motivation for giving up a significant part of one's life doing something that provides for the rest of one's life, food, clothing, shelter, and hopefully a holiday on occasion, instead of reaping the often larger financial rewards of for-profit sales and marketing (Do I sound snarky? Well maybe a little, but this is true).

Given that we in the for-profit and nonprofit worlds are not measuring the same things, it would follow that the ways we work, the processes of getting to our goals and meeting our mission, will probably reflect that difference; however, there is an ever-greater overlap between the methods of for-profits and nonprofits. Nonprofits are hiring advertising agencies to promote themselves. For-profits are emphasizing team creation. Nonprofits have more for-profit executives on nonprofit boards than ever before, and look to the for-profit sector for funding. For-profits have socially inclusive mission statements, are questioning traditional hierarchical structures, and are experimenting with values-based leadership. Work is being done to change laws to allow groups to operate as for-profit/nonprofit hybrids. It is a somewhat confusing time in the world of organizations and companies and actually, this is the stuff of a yet-to-be-written volume. So let's get back to nonprofit missions.

2.3 Defining Mission and Where That Definition Takes Us

What I often do before writing, essentially to make sure I know what I'm writing about, is to look up the meaning of the word or words about which I am writing in multiple English dictionaries, so that I can be sure I am understanding the accepted definition of the term, as well as its etymology. It is limiting because it reflects an English-speaking mindset, and I include this statement to be clear that there are other definitions of mission and this is just one way of looking at the concept.

In looking up "mission," I had an awakening moment: mission is a noun, as in "My organization's *mission* is to save the whales," and a transitive verb, as in "She is being sent on *mission.*" Mission comes from a Latin word *mittere,* meaning "to send." Missions, be it the buildings, the journeys, the labors, or the life callings, started with people involved in a religious order; one of the first uses of the word was by Jesuit missionaries, who used it to describe members of their order sent overseas to establish schools and churches. These structures were called missions (*Cambridge Dictionary,* 2016; *Merriam-Webster,* 2016; *Oxford English Dictionary,* 2016; Vocabulary.com, 2016).

Given the large number of definitions from different sources, I've reviewed and grouped the definitions into thematic areas as follows:

Mission as an assigned journey

- A special assignment that is given to a person or group.
- An important assignment carried out for political, religious, or commercial purposes, typically involving travel.

■ A body of persons sent to conduct negotiations or establish relations with a foreign country.

■ A body of experts or dignitaries sent to a foreign country.

Mission as deployment of military forces

■ A specific military or naval task or combat operation.

■ A flight by an aircraft or spacecraft to perform a specific task: a mission to the moon.

Mission as life purpose

■ An ambition or purpose that is assumed by a person or group, for example, a person who feels it is their mission in life to help the poor.

Organizational mission

■ A welfare or educational organization established for the needy people of a district.

■ The business with which such a body of persons is charged.

Religious mission

■ A body of persons sent to a foreign land by a religious organization, especially a Christian organization, to spread its faith or provide educational, medical, and other assistance.

■ The organized work of a religious missionary.

■ To organize or establish a religious mission among (a people) or in (an area).

■ An operation that is assigned by a higher headquarters.

Mission as a place

■ The district assigned to a mission worker.

■ A building or compound housing a mission.

■ A permanent diplomatic office abroad.

There are a number of things that immediately stood out to me as I pulled the definitions together, including the idea of a mission being important, high level, giving life meaning, special, involving travel, and as a location or structure. (I left out the military piece for multiple reasons including that we are talking about nonprofits, my Quaker practice, and my ongoing conviction that the military should not be involved in humanitarian or development efforts unless there is no other option—and there usually is another option.) Most definitions infer or state that the mission is decided upon and controlled by someone or someone's higher-up in a structure (God, the Drill Sargent, or your grandmother). Using the word "mission" to describe how organizations or corporations carry out work toward a vision brings with it potentially unexamined connotations that can impact how the mission is achieved.

Because we are discussing nonprofits, I have taken the liberty to distill the concepts included within mission into the following: mission implies a special, important purpose and/or journey undertaken by someone who is also special and important, and is based on a higher value decided on by one's superiors. Nonprofits also have offices and locations for service delivery; however, today they can be offices, store fronts, buildings, or tents, depending on the kind of work being done. People carrying out nonprofit work may believe they are working for something greater than themselves, that they have been chosen for this work because they are special, and there are people who know more and are in charge, telling them what to do to make that something happen.

I'm not saying that all nonprofits operate this way, or that it is even a conscious way nonprofit staff think; however, I am posing that systems created based on the origins of "mission" have an impact on how today's nonprofits are managed and structured, as well as on the people who choose this work—who the work attracts. The origination is a very northern/western construct for describing how to get to a goal, and does not resonate with much of the world. It is hierarchical, linear, and, if the word was first used by the Jesuits, Christocentric in its origins. In fact, a friend recently said of a country that was accepting refugees from Syria, "everyone there thinks people coming in from the west to help are missionaries."

In nonprofits, the vision and the mission are touchstones for our work and our accountability. If we are, knowingly or unconsciously, starting from a concept of mission that includes a top-down approach that essentially states that one group is special and has a higher calling, dividing the "helpers" from the "helped," the "saviors" from the "unsaved," we are starting from ideas that determine who is in charge, who does the work, and how they do it.

2.3.1 Special and Important

If mission-driven people are special and important, we must know something and be of value, right? We may be internally driven to help others, deciding to forgo the for-profit salaries, or maybe we are not too fond of the way capitalism has turned out. Perhaps someone may have told us we would serve a greater good by helping. Any of these reasons has the possibility of making us feel that we are special.

Someone has charged us (or we have charged ourselves) with doing something that, by definition, elevates us over those whom we are helping. If we were them, someone would be helping us, but since we are not them, we must be in some even slightly better position. We may have gone to college, or to graduate school, and have learned a great deal—and spent a lot of money doing it. Perhaps we have seen others helping and noticed the respect they received. Or we are committed to a specific philosophy. In fact, during my interviews for this book, nearly every person with whom I spoke stated that they came to nonprofit work because they wanted to help, be it people, the environment, or something else, and/or that they had a strong desire for social justice. One person said, "I never really considered doing corporate work just because there didn't seem to be as much of a direct connection with the kinds of things I wanted my life to be about."

We want to make people's lives better, to help women who are victims of domestic violence. We in the west/north have the resources to fly to Nepal or the Philippines or the Central African Republic to help in an emergency. This is great. Thank God there are people who want to do something in addition to making money, who hold values that are greater than a plush bottom line. But tell me, those of you in the nonprofit world, don't you look down—even a little—on those who have gone into the for-profit sector to make money? Maybe I'm the only one who divides the world between those on Wall Street and those digging bore holes (wells), who in my heart judges them as "less than," as not *really* caring, but I don't think so. (And I have. Sometimes with good reason, for example, the mortgage crisis, corruption in the Securities and Exchange Commission, record CEO bonuses after the 2008 collapse … please stop me now … and other times I'm just lumping everyone together—there are good people working in the finance industry that I know and respect as parents, partners, and humans—and make my prejudices somewhat unfair.) Which leads me to the idea that if we are doing nonprofit work without examining our own beliefs and motivations, particularly that we might be special and/or important, within existing structures and systems, we may be perpetuating the divisions in societies in ways that we have not thought of and are not helpful. And for those of us who have examined our motives—or been forced to examine them by experience—we know that it can hurt and can make us question why we ever got into this business in the first place.

* * *

I remember sitting alone at my desk at a social service agency in New York City after a particularly difficult meeting with a client. I was managing a team of six staff in a shelter setting; we worked with women who were homeless and had a major mental illness, to help them get ready to move to permanent housing with supportive services. During the meeting, my client was very angry with me because she didn't like the choices of housing she visited, and insisted on seeing more options. She was abrasive, demeaning, and dismissive. I was tired and frustrated and felt abused. Each staff person was tremendously committed from the Director down, we all worked long hours, spent significant time fighting medical bureaucracies so that the women received proper psychiatric and medical treatment, went up against government systems to obtain benefits to pay for housing, got legal help if the women needed it. The staff were passionate, completely committed to ensuring the women in the program succeeded and moved into housing.

After my client (who was really angry) left my office, I put my head in my hands thinking, "Why is she treating me like this? Why doesn't she understand I'm here to help her? That I have a really good idea of what's out there and where she would fit best? Why doesn't she appreciate all that I'm doing?"

And that was the moment, sitting with my head in my hands, feeling sorry for myself, that I realized that this work was not about me—at least not in the way that I thought. It wasn't about my client liking me, appreciating me and all my work, that I knew a lot about homelessness and mental illness and services and had an advanced degree and huge student loans and was special and important because of it. This was about her and her life and where she would live. It wasn't about me thinking I was great for doing all this helping, it was about all the fear and uncertainty and abuse and anger she had experienced prior to and living on the street and in shelters. It was about her finding a place where she felt safe, where she was not afraid. Where she wanted to live *her* life. In the big scheme of her life, I had very little to do with anything. That was when I understood how un-special and un-important I was in her schema, and that my work was actually about *that* woman getting housing in a place that worked for *her*; it was about being accountable to and respectful of her so that she could move forward. To allow her to be part of the decision-making system of creating her future, which had not been the case for much of her life. And because she was very clear about all of this, she provided me with the opportunity to examine my underlying assumptions of my role and my reasons for doing the work, and to change.

I thought I knew something. I had a lot of experience and information. I thought I knew why I went to school to be a social worker and why I was doing this work. I thought the satisfaction that came with helping others would be my reward because those people would like and appreciate me. That my guilt about being born into a white working-class family and never having missed a meal would be assuaged. That I would be special and important because I went to school not to get a Master's in Business Administration, but to get a Master's in Social Work and help others. Don't get me wrong, there is tremendous satisfaction in this work. The relationships you build, what you can learn, the great pay (not). But if, like me, your primary orientation is, "I'm helping! I'm going to help the homeless," you could be walking down the wrong path. You could be starting with the idea that someone can save some-one else and that you are the person doing the saving—and in some situations, that is true. In humanitarian emergencies, lives can be saved. People can be pulled from the rubble after an earthquake. Medical staff can provide medicines and treatment. Greenpeace and other environmental groups get between whales and whalers. These can be life-saving acts to be commended, but even in these situations, if one has the self-view as the "saver," the divide still exists; if we believe that we, and our institutions, are saving people or animals or the planet, we are coming at this from the wrong orientation. This is not to say that the work should stop, or that people should give up, or that you should not derive satisfaction from your work! On the contrary, this is not about giving up, but about thinking about how we do the work so that we are no longer needed—or there are many fewer of us needed because the world is filled with people who have had a voice in creating their world, from the day-to-day through international policy decision-making, causing the systems in which we currently operate to change. If we are successful in our work, isn't our ultimate goal, our primary mission, to get to the point where we are out of a job, and our organizations are no longer needed? One interviewee put it most succinctly when she said,

> What I would have liked to see happen, would have been families we were working with like graduating so to speak ... becoming independent, self-sufficient, saying I don't need your help anymore.

Another said,

> Ultimately that's what we want to see, that they can do the work on their own, that youth is not seen as a separate population, because they are underutilized, oftentimes not respected by others. We want to offer them the big vision. Part of that, since we are a facilitation and support role, is us not being necessary. If we're doing our job right, they should be able to empower themselves, and use their agency to do things without us. So success would be us putting ourselves out of business. The youth that we work with, we don't want to be required, because that breeds dependence. That is not what our mission is about. So I guess success would be doing such a good job at helping other people take action, we would not be needed.

The fact was that in my role at the shelter, I did know something. I knew about what existed in terms of provision of services for people who were homeless in New York City, I knew the phone numbers of the housing providers, I knew some of them personally. I knew what I had learned in my coursework and in my experience. But I wasn't listening well enough. I needed to move into a space of what I like to call "not knowing," of holding what I knew while at the same time opening up enough to hear what my client knew, learned, and experienced, and to experience that she, too, was special and important and had just as much right to feel that way as I did. She was helping herself. We had another meeting, we talked again about what she needed/wanted, and, after setting up a few more tours and getting a lot but not all of what she wanted, she was able to decide on a living space where she felt comfortable, safe, and supported. *That* was success.

In nonprofit workplaces we are all special, and we are all important, and at the same time we are all replaceable. That's the fact. It's good to remember this, because it links our individuality with humility.*

2.3.2 Higher Calling

Many of us working in nonprofits are in it because we are interested in a better world. We are doing this work for the greater good, not primarily for ourselves—although there are benefits to each of us if the ozone layer is not depleted, and if soil remains fit to grow our food.

The idea of higher calling stems from the origin of the idea of mission, that there is someone or something (God, humanity, elephants, trees) that has some inherent meaning for each of us. Meaning is that which is intended to be through words,

---

* This is true in many northern/western cultures, the idea of the individual as separate from the group. Just another thing to think about when managing at work.

actions, or writing, the outcome, the sense you make of what another is saying or doing (*Oxford English Dictionary*, 2016).

It is one of the things that makes us human, our desire to make meaning (sense) out of the world around us. And although I am only a lowly social worker writing a book on management, based on my experience I can say that there are probably as many different meanings for Life, the Universe, and Everything (Adams, 1982) as there are people on the planet. Joseph Campbell said that "life is without meaning, you bring the meaning to it, the meaning … is whatever you ascribe it to be. Being alive is meaning."* Victor Frankl (1959) wrote, "the meaning of life differs from man to man, from day to day and from hour to hour. What matters, therefore, is not the meaning of life in general but rather the specific meaning of a person's life at a given moment." Tolstoy (1894) wrote, "The sole meaning of life is to serve humanity by contributing to the establishment of the kingdom of God, which can only be done by the recognition and profession of the truth by every man.".

I would hazard to say that the meaning people create moves them to take certain paths in their lives. For the Jesuits, the meaning comes from their belief in and commitment to Jesus Christ. All of their work follows from that, schools, universities, evangelization. For Nelson Mandela, meaning came from his belief in the equality of all people and his resulting commitment to put an end to apartheid in South Africa (Nelson Mandela Foundation, 2016). For Susan B. Anthony it was her Quaker beliefs and experience of exclusion from the Temperance movement that led her to campaign for women's right to vote (National Susan B. Anthony Museum and House, 2013). Each has been considered as having a higher calling, engaged in work and/or processes benefiting more than the individual or the individual's family or group.

There is supposed to be little personal gain in a higher calling (other than the idea of going to Heaven), and there can

---

* This quote is ascribed to a lecture given by Joseph Campbell.

be great sacrifice in responding to something greater, as in the murder of the Reverend Dr. Martin Luther King, and President Mandela's long imprisonment. In the Christian and Muslim worlds, responding to a higher calling is linked with being rewarded in "the next life," being allowed entrance to Heaven. Problems start when people are led to believe that one higher calling is more important than all others; this is a perversion of higher calling and is a cover for the acquisition of power or for the satisfaction of sadists, whether by suicide bombings or the Inquisition.

We live in a very uncertain world. In fact, we have little promise that we will exist beyond the current moment. It's like all of us are walking on a path and with every step the road is rising to meet us and one day we'll take a step and the road will not be there and we will cease to be. We live forever on the edge of uncertainty, and most days it's just too much to deal with given the pile of dishes in the sink, the morning commute, the field that needs to be harvested. It's beyond scary, it infuses everything we do, think, say. We can't regularly acknowledge it because we'd never get anything done. We'd always have to be asking ourselves, "wow, will making this breakfast actually matter because I might not be here in a moment?," or it may trigger depression, or bad decision-making (bungee jumping/cave diving/eating at McDonalds). It's too much for most of us mortals, and so we have developed belief systems to help us cope.

Belief systems, which I think precede meaning, are based on these deep-seated terrors. It may be one of the reasons that antidepressant use is so high—with the diminishment of participation in formal religion, people don't have the guideposts provided by religious belief and may realize that we are essentially making this all up as we go. Terrifying.

Traditionally, the flip side of terror/fear that has been created to subdue the fear is the promise of something better at another time (Heaven/ice cream), which leads to hope; that if my situation is terrible now, it can be better in the future, a better world for me and my children, for people living in drought conditions in the Sahel. So we act, hoping to alleviate our fears, often without an examination of what is actually moving us to act. This is not true universally—there are people who have examined their fears and have acted from a position of clarity and strength: Rosa Parks. Gandhi. Malala. For most of us, though, this is not the case.

Some of us try to alleviate our fears by earning a great deal of money. Others alleviate that fear by giving to the NRA Foundation (mission: "preserving the core of our American values and traditions in our steadfast effort to Teach Freedom"— you'd never know it was about guns). Or by throwing ourselves into responding to disasters. Or by building houses through Habitat for Humanity, or by mediating conflicts.

The fact is that almost everyone on the planet is operating from the same starting place: we are afraid, primarily of no longer existing. It's one of the things, like breathing, that we all have in common. And the same is true for hope, because without hope, we don't have much reason to go on.

In *The Persistence of Subjectivity: On the Kantian Aftermath*, Robert Pippin writes that the "classes" in the late nineteenth and early twentieth centuries were "suspended between hope and fear, the hope for ascent and the fear of sinking back into the working class" (2005). Bringing us to the downside of the hope/fear dyad. And please know that I am all for hope—I just think we have to hold it close, figure out what it means, and then think about how to get there. With others. Because if we are all "I me mine," we become shareholders in life instead of stakeholders.

If we base our decisions on hope and/or fear, *we leave a lot to chance* (the devil you know is better than the devil you don't, I hope one day to see Paris, you get the idea). The good news is that if most of us are operating from this starting place, we have something in common. And if this is the case, how do we acknowledge it and use it to bridge the differences in belief and meaning that we have made? How do we acknowledge the things that we have in common, as well as the different ways we have created to deal with our fear/hope conundrum? How do we move beyond the hope/fear paradigm so that we can work toward an outcome that is based on what is in front of us instead of what we believe? Because if each of us is convinced that our belief system, and the meaning we have made from it, is the best way to alleviate fear and provide hope, we are only contributing to and exacerbating the fear, and muting the hope, that lives within others.

If our "higher calling" is the best one, if we are convinced of that, then we are making others more afraid and less hopeful. And if our higher calling and the way we carry it out is unexamined, the path we take to get to the goal of higher calling—in the case of nonprofits, the mission—is actually based on an existing premise and system and becomes unknowingly tainted. If you are "right" and the other is "wrong," you may act in ways that do not acknowledge and respect the other as another human being. And this defeats the whole process of creating a better world.

2.3.3 Decided upon by Higher-Ups

Growing up, most of us realize from a young age that there are people who know more than we do. Every parent—or anyone who has been around a toddler—knows that one of the first words they learn, and love, is NO. There is a great deal of self-efficacy in the ability to refuse something, be it a certain food, a bath, or going to bed. Contrarily, children also love structure. They will rebel against it through crying, stomping, head-shaking, and saying NO, but ultimately children feel secure when they know the rhythms of life and can depend on them. (I realize this is a gross generalization, that some children are fine without structure, that sometimes structure is *too* structured, that some will say that this maintains the status quo, but I'm making a point—wait for it …).

There is security in believing that there are others who know more than we do and can keep us safe. It's a scary and also fascinating world, and it has really helped us to survive as a species by having people who know more than we do both protect and encourage us, watching to make sure we explore our environment but not allowing us to stick our hand in a cobra hole or see what lovely blue window cleaner tastes like. It's less scary when you have someone who is going to keep you safe. If you have grown up in a situation where no one has kept you safe, or someone has made the world unsafe, such as in situations of abuse (physical/sexual/emotional) or abandonment, or the world around you is unsafe as some children experience in war zones, you have had to figure out ways to keep yourself safe. This can lead to different ways of thinking about how the world works and can impact your behavior and coping mechanisms. Or you may be physically safe and raised in a specific way with rigid strictures about being seen in public, or attending school, or what a higher power accepts as good versus bad behavior and thoughts.

Those "in the know," those creating the structures, are often seen as higher-up. And it has led to hierarchies. Hierarchies are all around us. Hierarchy theory is an academic discipline, a component of general systems theory. Biological science is based on hierarchy, as is the human body, mathematics, and physics (Allen, 2001). We see hierarchies in our families, our communities, our countries, and we are impacted by living within and being taught these systems. They are in some ways fundamental to helping us make sense of the world, and they also offer us some grounding, establishing order, providing us a place in the big scheme of things.

The problem comes in when we conflate hierarchy in the natural world with hierarchies based on belief systems created by human beings. Before the 1928 Representation of the People Act, women under 20 in the UK were not allowed to vote (Whitfield, 2001), based on the belief that men were superior to women in their intelligence and decision-making, and that women could not be trusted with the franchise. Or when a person is born into the Dalit caste in India, outside of the Varnas of Brahmins, Kshatriyas, Vaisyas, and Sudras, and cannot move from her/his level no matter their gifts or abilities; the idea is that being born into the Dalit is a punishment for wrongs in a previous life. Both of these examples are based on hierarchies decided by the beliefs of by the beliefs of one or more people in a system that exercises power and control, and is without the input of those impacted by the results of those beliefs.

From a U.S.–European Christocentric perspective, a white, bearded all-knowing God sits at the head of everything. His son, Jesus, said "I am the way and the truth and the life, no one comes to the father but through me." Given that the idea and implementation of "mission" came from the Jesuits, and *their* mission is to ask the following in all aspects of their lives: "What have I done for Christ? What am I doing for Christ? What will I do for Christ?," it is clear that belief and meaning, in the history of the idea of mission, held God as the "highest" higher-up, Jesus Christ as the next highest higher-up, then a whole raft of angels and saints and I just don't know enough to continue along this line. Mary fits in somewhere. Then we have an intermediary between all of those folks and regular mortals: the priest/minister/reverend/your choice here _____. The mortals are at the bottom of the heap.

The implication is that there is a human person, an intermediary, who knows more than everyone else and has a more direct line to God and Jesus/the higher power than the average person. And because of this, that person has the God-given (pun intended) right to instruct and/or direct others in what God wants them to do. And then, as in the Inquisition, someone higher-up can decide that if you are not a believer, you need to come to believe or be killed in horrific ways. Or shunned. Or not receive things that come along with believing. Even in the recent past, there have been reported cases of the exchange of food for religious conversion, both by governments (U.S. Department of State, 2011) and by religious groups or their representatives who have used food and other incentives to encourage people to convert (Gartland, 2009; Manuel et al., 2006). However, in most cases today, nonprofits are guided by national and international laws and internal codes of conduct which are in place to preclude these types of behaviors. And given Pope Francis' statements and writings, I think we're moving toward a much more inclusive outlook, at least from the Catholic church.

Religious hierarchy impacted governance structures. In Europe, monarchies developed from the idea of a Christian God sitting at the head of everything; the culture was such that this was accepted by the nobility—especially by the nobility—and those around them (Ikram, 2006). Eons prior, Egypt's monarchs were god-kings, a merger of the human and the divine. China's governance, by and large, looked to Confucianism (more of a social and ethical philosophy than a religion) as its model for government structures and policies (Goucher et al., 1998).

As religious beliefs changed, governance structures and hierarchies, and command and control also changed; when Martin Luther apocryphally nailed his *Disputation of Martin Luther on the Power and Efficacy of Indulgences* to the door of the Catholic Church and translated the Christian Bible into the vernacular of the day, Christianity morphed and moved from the Pope as the highest direct contact with and ultimate authority on God. And although Catholicism is still strong around the world, there are also varying Christian sects: Lutherans, Methodists, Presbyterians, and, at the far end of the reformation spectrum, the Unitarian Universalists, a group that has no dogma or doctrine but holds Seven Principles including justice, equality, passion, democratic processes, and peace that are drawn from Six Sources, including personal experience and Jewish, Christian, humanistic, and spiritual teachings. Some Unitarian Universalists believe in God, others do not (Unitarian Universalist Association, 2016).

In the U.S. and Europe, governance moved from monarchy* to democratic governance structures. Although there is still significant power in the hands of the president or prime minister (after all, George W. Bush was "The Decider"), there is a recognition that there can be sense and wisdom in the populace, and that it is helpful that the citizens, the ones contributing to and benefiting from government, are included in how and what policy decisions are made, and in who represents them to make those decisions. The structure and process of democratic government, in many cases but certainly not all,† follows the beliefs and meaning of those it represents. There are bodies in Berlin or Santiago or Lusaka that have been elected and who make decisions and should represent the will of those who elected them, bringing the idea of "decision-making by higher-ups" down a few notches.

Which begs the question: *Who in your nonprofit organization has the closest link to God?* I'm just kidding (mostly …), but if we are not examining the basis of this idea and its impact on how we see the world and our place in it, we could be unconsciously recreating the top-down power dynamics (and the striving to move up the nonprofit ladder) that got us to where we are today both in nonprofits as well as in the larger world.

If nonprofit organizations are based on a mission, and the mission is decided upon by people who, consciously or unconsciously, see themselves as a group differentiated from the "other," we may be helping to feed or clothe or vaccinate someone, which is great, and at the same time we may be enforcing the essentially divisive system that makes

---

* Although some monarchs are the titular Head of State, such as in the UK.
† By "not all," I am referring to countries that are authoritarian in nature but contain the word "democratic" in their names.

"charitable" provision of these things necessary. Why not a world where people are able to access the things they need in a way that ensures dignity? Those on the receiving end of nonprofit work are most often not those making decisions about what is needed and how it should be prioritized and delivered, what is valued and what is not.

2.4 Summary

Wow! There are going to be quite a few nonprofit workers who are really angry with me right now. I can hear it: "That's not me! I'm in this for the right reasons, I'm not doing this because I have some deep-seated fear or insecurity about the afterlife! I don't think I'm better than everyone! I'd never say I was (a) god! I have to tell people what to do because otherwise how would they know? Why are you saying all these terrible things?! I've seen suffering and I understand it and I want to help. I've lived it and I know it and I can make a difference. It's the system that's a mess!"

I believe you. Well, most of you. And the system *is* a mess.

I've dissected mission because if you ask anyone in the development or humanitarian world, or in the nonprofit world more generally, they will tell you about the problems they face in reaching their mission. The long-term "stays" for what should be short-term emergency responses. The dilemmas in ending programs and/or leaving communities because there is money to continue, or the money runs out. The power imbalances. The money that flows to humongous development and relief organizations where staffs are required by government-provided grants to fly only on national airlines even if it is more expensive, or import supplies made in the country where the grant is issued even if the same supplies may be available locally and for a lower cost. Organizations spending funds on ad agencies to increase brand recognition to compete for more grants and more contracts with the consequence of sustaining the organization becoming an end in itself. And because so many nonprofits in the development and humanitarian world are northern/western based, they are staffed, at least in headquarters, by people who feel special and important because they are working for a higher calling, and they are told what to do by higher-ups, who feel special and important because *they* are working for a higher calling. And not unlike the for-profit sector, there are people in those organizations who are afraid. Afraid they will not reach the mission. Afraid they will not meet their goals (personal and professional). Afraid the money will run out. Afraid they will lose their job. And on the other hand, they are hopeful, generally about the same things. Which, as I indicated before, leaves a lot to chance.

I've dissected mission also because I have come to think that those of us working in nonprofits in the north/west need to consider what it means to be in a management structure that could be seen as a blend of Christian/parental beliefs and meanings, even if it does not manifest as monarchical or "Big Brother." If we are managing within a mission that has been decided by higher-ups, if the organization has a one-way method of information dissemination—top-down—then we are missing the point of social change; we are creating fixed-solution programs that are determined by one (or a few) possibly out-of-touch person(s) with a specific agenda looking for a specific outcome. Voila! We have the Iraq war. Which, by the way, was not started by a nonprofit.

The rules/systems/processes for development and humanitarian work, as well as work in many national and local nonprofits, have come from the north and west, and this is why we need to look at how we define mission. That the residual traces of that definition might linger is quite crucial, because if we are working (including managing) *to achieve* the mission, which is the essence of why nonprofits exist, we may not be looking at the historical forces that impact our reasons for doing the work and managing our organizations, and those forces have consequences. They have consequences in our behaviors and in our actions, which directly affects how we interact with one another inside our organizations, as well as with those the organization is intended to serve. Some people will say that it matters less how we do the work, that as long as we are getting results, it's ok, we don't *really* need to look inward or at the origins of the nonprofit world, we are grounded in faith/knowledge/data/and so on, and we really do have *the* answer. And that makes me more than sad, it makes me angry.

If we in the not-for-profit sector are focused on mission, and the mission has historic roots in a specific structure—in this case top-down—then we have an implicit if unexamined way to structure and manage our organizations, and that is top-down. Higher calling, run from above. Staff do what they are told, and those whom the organization is serving get what is given.

An example of this top-down decided by higher-ups approach was work being done with girls and women who had been raped as a weapon of war. Although it is not their fault in any way, almost all women feel some sense of shame associated with being raped. In a number of cultures, if a woman has been raped, she is no longer marriageable and becomes an outcast in her community. In some cultures, a girl/woman who has been raped will be killed for bringing shame on her family. Or she has seen what happens to other women who report rapes to authorities and never talks about it. If we have been told by our higher-ups that setting up a place for women who have been raped to go and talk about their situation, in a traditional psychotherapeutic manner, is the best intervention, we would probably follow their direction, and get to work. Or maybe that videotaping women who have been raped and using the video to raise awareness (and maybe also for fundraising), we may feel that our desire to help is enough. And we may put women's lives in danger by revealing their rape to the community or to a government bent on keeping rape as a weapon of war against a minority population a secret.

In the aforementioned interventions, there is an idea that someone outside the situation knows something and can fix the "problem," that the person has a higher calling to help women who have been raped, and that the intervention, the way the help is delivered, has been decided outside of the impacted community, without asking what the people in the community think would work, or what has worked historically. This is fraught with uncertainty; we may be under direct "orders" to do it in the prescribed way. Our funders may be expecting us to carry out the work exactly as described in a grant. Or we may be afraid to step outside of what we know because we know it, and it makes us special and important. And separate.

As someone who was accompanied by a video team during an international assessment mission, I was complicit in interviewing a girl who had been raped; this young woman was part of a group, and she surprised us by talking about it. The interview was recorded and shown at a later time. And I am deeply, profoundly ashamed. I have no excuses, although it is very hard to tell your higher-ups and media people what you think if it is not what they want to hear.

If we stop acting in a traditional top-down/directed from above/"I'm helping" manner, we might look at ways of working with women and girls who have been raped that have been undertaken in other crises. Getting to know and talking with community gatekeepers may mean that an original idea or plan may need to be changed, or scrapped. It might be decided that creating a space for young moms to come together in the interest of their children, for feeding or play or education, and letting them discuss issues as they see fit, is a non-overt way to work to reduce traumatization. Or another intervention might be suggested by women in the community. This embraces the idea of an evolving, process-driven mission, one that partners with those traditionally on the receiving end and has at least a little bit of space for change.

* * *

If, as nonprofit workers, managers, leaders, we are buoyed by the idea of seeing ourselves as special, responding to a higher calling and being directed by higher-ups, we will carry on as we have always done. But at some point, if we believe we are special and important, and decisions as to our work are being made somewhere else, outside of ourselves, this might chafe our self-opinion. At some point we might wonder when *we* are higher-up enough to make the decisions. Which is a repercussion of not being included and, unfortunately, trickles down to those whom the organization serves often being seen as without the capacity for "good" decision-making and therefore without input into problem-solving. And then the people being served, who have self-efficacy, will start to wonder when *they* get to make the decisions. It's like one of those houses of mirrors at a carnival when you were a kid; reflection after reflection of the same image to infinity with no actual change.

Mission is a critical concept, but needs to be as much *process-driven* as goal-driven. The processes of inclusion, listening, equity, and acknowledgment. The processes of the creation of structures, systems, and managing. The idea that we don't and can't know it all, that everyone has a piece of the puzzle of this world, and that we need to acknowledge that, just because we in the north and west have resources and knowledge, it does not make us special; in reality, it just makes it harder to connect to those who are not like us. If we want to change the way the world looks, if we want to ensure greater equity, we may have to reformulate vision and mission within the context of how we see ourselves and how the work gets done, which I'm calling the "process." Do we want a process that replicates the status quo? Or do we want a process in which change includes everyone? Where the lines between helper and helped are diminished?

Although we may not be able to make huge systemic change, those of us in nonprofits have the capacity to make change toward a greater balance in our own organizations, within ourselves, our staffs, and the people with whom we are working. We can distinguish ourselves from altruistic private sector mission statements through the addition of a "process statement," including values and a Code of Ethics, that guides all aspects of how the organization works, including how people manage. These can be decided on by those in the organization doing the work and, hopefully, the board and the people being served, to achieve the vision and mission. At the very least, reconceptualizing "mission" can nudge people working in nonprofits to start a conversation about how people in the organization will work together to achieve the mission and vision. At best, the act of creating process, values, and ethics statements, and its application to managing, can be a disruptor* of "business as usual," lessening power divides and even cracking the hope/fear paradigm through transparent, inclusive policies, roles, and planning.

In the nonprofit world, we are not limited to how many nails we can produce or how much money our corporation earns; we are concerned with change for the good of all. We can decide, through the development of a process statement and its application to how we manage, to create a world reflected in the Starbucks mission: to *inspire and nurture the human spirit—one person, one cup and one neighborhood at a time.* Well, maybe not the cup part, but you get the idea.

---

* Although I really dislike this word, managing as mission presents an opportunity for everyone to be "disruptive," not just an elite few.

Chapter III

Process

Science is the process that takes us from confusion to understanding.

Brian Greene

Thank goodness for science. It provides a way for us to make sense out of our world and ourselves. We no longer have to worry that fleas will spontaneously emerge from the dust in our homes, that miasma creates illness, or that earthquakes are the wrath of God made manifest. We have a way to understand—and subsequently to create and take actions that might actually address—problems we face, because we know the etiology of those problems. We have come up with doggie flea shampoo and the "elbow sneeze," and we can construct buildings that can flex with the shifting of the earth. Each of these solutions followed a process of investigation; from one person or a group deciding that the conventional idea of causality might not be the *actual* cause, coming up with other possibilities, then testing them to determine whether their new ideas held water. From there, solutions can be developed by those original ideators/testers, and/or by others picking up on the new thinking and creating solutions through ideating and testing.

Without those individuals and groups who had new ideas and who worked to test them, we would be drinking from *E. coli*-infested waters, dropping like flies from cholera, and wondering what we were doing wrong to make God hate us so much that he/she made the earth shake.

In primary school, science was a subject where we learned about rocks, clouds, plants, illness, fish, oceans, and a raft of other seemingly dissociated things. When we got to high school, science became biology, chemistry, and physics. In college, classes further defined science as meteorology, anatomy and physiology, nutrition, biochemistry, calculus, you get the idea. First we learned the general, then we drilled down to greater specificity because there is just so darn much to know in any one area. Perhaps we went through a process to get to be an engineer or a doctor or a quantum physicist; learning, thinking, testing, starting over, retesting, and if we were on the right track, we might come up with proof for our new idea. Then it would be peer reviewed and published in a scientific journal. It's a process. It takes time. And there is an acknowledgment that even if something was thought to be true, once it is proved false, (hopefully) the world moves on to look for some other idea. Or, if a tested hypothesis turns into a proven theory, we face a new set of questions. Walt Whitman wrote,

> Now understand me well—it is provided in the essence of
> things that from any fruition of
> success, no matter what, shall come forth something
> to make a greater struggle
> necessary (1900).

And although I agree with Dr. Greene, who provided the quote to open this chapter, regarding science leading us from confusion to understanding, I think that there are many ways—processes—to get from confusion to understanding. Science is one. Walt Whitman's poetry is another. Dialogue is a third. It is the point at which you start, the reason you desire to move from confusion to understanding that makes the difference: there has to be a *fundamental desire to understand, and a willingness to be wrong*. An acknowledgment that we might be confused. Or have an idea that does not make sense. Or, in reality, don't have a clue. But we have to *want* to understand.

A person can approach getting from confusion to understanding in many ways, depending on how one was raised, one's neural wiring, experiences, culture, physical environment. As stated previously, we as humans have a deep need to make sense of our world. For some of us, making sense of things comes from science, where testing and retesting is the norm. For others, religion helps to make sense of things and provides rules on how we are supposed to behave, including interacting with others. Science and religion are not necessarily mutually exclusive; in many religions and sects, science is fully embraced (as with the Jesuits and their deep commitment to research and education—I needed to cut them a little slack as Mendel, Teilhard de Chardin, and Lemaître were all Jesuits). However, belief being equated with science, for example the idea that Jesus rode dinosaurs and that, according to some interpretations of the Christian Bible, the world is about 6000 years old, is problematic for me given that it goes against evidence from multiple scientific disciplines. People can believe that the Bible is literal, the truth (the whole truth and nothing but the truth, so help me God) (I couldn't resist), but implicit in this is a disregard of empirical evidence and a desire to shun the ideas and theories of others. Groups committed to one way of thinking at the exclusion of others, be it based in religion, national identity, or culture, have found their understanding and no longer seek anything else. Certainty is valued, and being wrong is not an option.

We might understand our world through a profound relationship with our environment; Iroquois First Nations people tell of a time of water, when there was no ground. A sky woman fell through a hole in the sky, and the animals saved her from drowning by building the Earth on the back of a turtle. The creatures created the Earth so that the sky woman could live; those same creatures supplied First Nations people with food and skins, and nothing went to waste. There was, and still is, the sense of deep connection to and valuing of the earth, the sky and all things connected to the earth and sky (Native Languages of the Americas, 2015).

If one is born into a stratified society, one might understand the world and their place in it through that stratification. The ancient Egyptians had such a society, with the Pharaoh at the top and the slaves at the bottom. They believed that in the after-life, Pharaohs rose up to ride across the sky with the sun god Re to protect the world and Egypt. And to ensure the Pharaohs had what was needed to get to and flourish in the afterlife, they were buried with all they might need, including, sometimes, pets and servants. It was thought that the servants would have a great time in the afterlife because they would be with the Pharaoh and Re—although I imagine no one asked the servants what they thought (Ikram, 2006). Protection, wealth, and a connection with a god were important. These things were valued.

Getting from confusion to understanding, in great part, relies on one's values and beliefs; it's where you start. It involves trust, that through your desire and the desire of others to authentically understand something via science, debate, poetry, insert your chosen methodology _____, and that alone and with others you will arrive at a helpful, useful understanding that makes sense of the world. It involves relationships between people, structures, systems, and so on. And it mandates a process be used, an authentic process, which may or may not result in the outcomes one wanted, evoking uncertainty and the possibility of change.

In this chapter, we will explore the ways in which ideas, beliefs, and values manifest both in how nonprofit workers think about the mission and their work, as well as in the behaviors that come from ideas, beliefs, and values. If staff values lack consistency throughout the organization, this can lead to misunderstandings and less productive work; working together to create a Values Statement and Code of Ethics can help staff gain clarity. The chapter concludes by suggesting that the additional step of staff development of a Process Statement—an agreed-upon understanding of how the work is done, or the means and how those means are reflective of the mission/world we want—is incredibly helpful both inside the organization and when conveying the organization's purpose and work to stakeholders. By the end of this chapter, your organization will be able to develop a Values Statement, a Code of Ethics, and a Process Statement.

3.1 Ideas, Beliefs, Values, and Behaviors

Values. We all have them. They are the worth, the weight we give to our ideas and beliefs. Values arise from a desire to prioritize those beliefs so that we can make sense of the world, and to provide a common/communal/codified foundation for dealing with our environment that works to link us to one another. Or to separate us, depending on your beliefs and how they inform your values and subsequent behaviors. By prioritizing our ideas and beliefs, we are establishing, to the best of our abilities, our place in the great cosmic soup,* and providing guidance as to the behaviors that allow us to live together (or not). My husband says that happiness comes from synchronizing your life with your values.

Values come from the ideas we create or latch onto in our attempts to make sense of our environment, our life experiences, and the experiences of those around us. And they are invisible, unless you are a hipster, then the hat, tattoos, and facial hair establish you as a very, very cool person who values coolness. Values might also be visible if you decide to open carry a rifle in a store; if you are doing this because you value security, might I suggest moving to rural Alaska where

---

* Thanks to Carl Sagan.

you wouldn't have to worry so much. Other than about the bears. Big, big bears.

In his article, "Basic Human Values: Theory, Methods, and Applications," Shalom H. Schwartz (2006: 37–38) describes how people prioritize values based on how they adapt to experiences in their lives:

> Adaptation may take the form of upgrading attainable values and downgrading thwarted values. But the reverse occurs with values that concern material well-being and security.

Because values come from ideas and beliefs arising out of adaptation to life experiences, the culture into which we were born thrusts values upon each of us from the moment we leave the womb. Our neural circuitry also impacts how we make sense out of the world, as does our ongoing interaction with our environment. Until we can begin to put ideas together for ourselves, our values are often outside our control and may not be the values we ultimately hold. Or there may be dissonance between the value system in which we grew up and who we realize we are; we might have been raised in a family or community that does not value education, and have an innate curiosity, a hunger for knowledge. This dissonance can lead to great frustration if one attempts to conform by squelching that curiosity, or, if one decides to "rebel" and learn things either via school or on one's own, it can lead to a break with family or the community or, as a positive outcome, it may lead to a change in the values of the community.

In some countries and cultures, due to mores and gender role assignment, the idea of educating girls is seen as a waste of resources and a drain on the family;* if a child is going to

---

* Thankfully, this is changing due to international and national commitments; in 2003, UNICEF reported that 61M primary-school-aged girls were out of school (2003), in contrast to 31M in 2013 as reported by UNESCO (2013). This is still 31M too many.

be sent to school, it will be the boy who will eventually need to earn a living to support his family. Girls will get married and have children, and they won't need education. In the 1900s, this was still true in developed as well as developing countries. Like in the U.S.

My mother's sister Hazel, born between 1900 and 1905, was really smart. She was the oldest of six girls and, in a family story, on the day of her primary-school graduation the school Principal pulled her father (my grandfather) aside, to tell him that Hazel was a great candidate for high school and possibly college. The story went that my grandfather turned to the Principal and said, "yes, yes, we'll enroll her next week," and as soon as the Principal walked away he turned to Hazel and said, "Forget about school; you're going to work on Monday." She did. And at least three of her sisters followed suit; I have a tin of buttons from her sisters Myrtle and Helen, they both left school and worked in "the button factory."

My grandfather lived in a world where women got married and had children at young ages. They went to work in factories or cleaned houses, which, to him, did not call for education. He could not see what we see now: that educating all children is a human right; that educated girls marry later and have fewer children; and those children are more likely to survive. Educated girls will earn more over their lifetimes and are more likely than their male counterparts to invest income into family and children (UNICEF, 2014).

By the time my mother was in school—she was a "change of life baby" (terminology of the time) and born in the late 1920s, 13 years after her next-oldest sister—my grandfather had a change in life circumstances that led to a change in values. Or maybe he was just exhausted after raising five girls. The world had changed, the Depression was over, all the other sisters were out of the home, and his living situation had improved. My mother attended and graduated from high school.

My grandfather's basic needs had been satisfied, he
had risen in Maslow's Hierarchy from the cusp between
Physiological and Safety to the cusp between Safety and Love/
Belonging. His values changed based on his life experience,
which allowed his thinking and actions to change. And my
mother had a better life because of it, as did my brother and I.

Values, although a way to weight and prioritize beliefs and
ideas, are not immutable.

Thankfully, there is an internationally agreed-upon set
of values created within the most widely acknowledged,
accepted, and representative international body, the United
Nations (UN). These values supersede things like keeping girls
out of school, torturing prisoners of war, and slavery, no matter your ideas, values, or culture. In the Preamble to the UN
Charter, the founders stated:

WE THE PEOPLES OF THE UNITED NATIONS DETERMINED

- to save succeeding generations from the scourge
  of war, which twice in our lifetime has brought
  untold sorrow to mankind, and
- to reaffirm faith in fundamental human rights,
  in the dignity and worth of the human person,
  in the equal rights of men and women and of
  nations large and small, and
- to establish conditions under which justice and
  respect for the obligations arising from treaties
  and other sources of international law can be
  maintained, and
- to promote social progress and better standards
  of life in larger freedom,

AND FOR THESE ENDS

- to practice tolerance and live together in peace
  with one another as good neighbours, and

- to unite our strength to maintain international peace and security, and
- to ensure, by the acceptance of principles and the institution of methods, that armed force shall not be used, save in the common interest, and
- to employ international machinery for the promotion of the economic and social advancement of all peoples (United Nations, 1945).

They are also codified in the Preamble to the Universal Declaration of Human Rights:

Whereas recognition of the inherent dignity and of the equal and inalienable rights of all members of the human family is the foundation of freedom, justice and peace in the world, Whereas disregard and contempt for human rights have resulted in barbarous acts which have outraged the conscience of mankind, and the advent of a world in which human beings shall enjoy freedom of speech and belief and freedom from fear and want has been proclaimed as the highest aspiration of the common people, Whereas it is essential, if man is not to be compelled to have recourse, as a last resort, to rebellion against tyranny and oppression, that human rights should be protected by the rule of law, Whereas it is essential to promote the development of friendly relations between nations, Whereas the peoples of the United Nations have in the Charter reaffirmed their faith in fundamental human rights, in the dignity and worth of the human person and in the equal rights of men and women and have determined to promote social progress and better standards of life in larger freedom (United Nations, 1948).

The underlying values within these documents include peace and security; the inherent dignity and worth of the human being; equality of men and women (and if you include the Convention on the Rights of the Child, children too); justice and the rule of law; social progress; tolerance; freedom of speech and belief and from fear and want; and equitable standards of living. They provide the baseline for international values; ideally, we as an international community, nation by nation, should be aiming to exceed these rights because as nations, we are only as good as our people and people, by existing, have rights.

For the past 25 years, the World Values Survey has conducted research in over 100 countries, measuring the weight of specific values in order to a. determine changes in values and b. determine correlation between values and societal changes, for example, economic growth, increase in women's rights, increase in democratic institutions (World Values Survey, 2016). Their findings have shown that variation in human values can lie anywhere between two dyads: traditional versus secular-rational and survival versus self-expression—people move from traditional (religious, respect for authority, obedience) to secular-rational (individual rights, inclusion, etc.) when their sense of existential security increases; and from survival to self-expression when their sense of individual agency increases (Inglehart and Welzel, 2005). Values can and do change and, subsequently, the behaviors associated with values change.

There are websites with lists and lists of values—hundreds of values—and in an attempt to provide a benchmark for understanding and measuring values, Schwartz et al. (2001) have consolidated these hundreds into 10 human values: Power; Achievement; Hedonism; Stimulation; Self-direction; Universalism; Benevolence; Tradition; Conformity; Security. Each of these values can be clustered into one of four "relationships," with ideas and behaviors stemming from those relationships. And within each of us, they are prioritized by our adaptation to life experiences. The relationships move one toward a view of self and a subsequent way of interacting with

Figure 3.1   Theoretical model of relations among 10 motivational types of values. (Reprinted with permission from *Revue Française de Sociologie* (2006), 47, no. 4 : 9).

the world: self-enhancement, openness to change, conservation, and self-transcendence, as depicted in Figure 3.1.

So many values! And we have not begun to consider the values included within values, as in, if I am a person who grew up in the suburbs and prioritizes safety/security as a value, I may subsequently value rural areas where there may be less crime but a lot of bears (Alaska?). And then I may operationalize those values by moving to a rural area and joining a local gun club after I buy a shotgun. JUST KIDDING! I might buy a good deadbolt lock and lock the front door at night, or join a local conservation group to preserve the land from wacky development. If I value safety/security and am a politician, I may vote to increase military spending. Or I could opt to increase international development spending on peacebuilding programs in schools. It's the ways in which we decide to manifest the values we hold that can bring about a better world or create profound alienation or nuclear annihilation. Values lead to behaviors, and behaviors have impact on others.

In the nonprofit world, there is often a belief, an assumption that we are operating from the same values in the same priority order; we think people engaged in nonprofit work tend to fall into the Self-Transcendence quadrant, focusing on benevolence and universalism. Again, most of the people I interviewed for this book indicated that they went into nonprofit work either because they wanted to "help" or because they saw injustice/inequity and wanted to work for justice and equity. They said, "I tried a number of things and I realized I'm one of those people who likes to help others," they were "inspired by social justice ideas, ideas of equality ... ideas of there being more compassion in the world ... to connect to what I wanted my life to be about," and they "had this idea that the inequity in the world shouldn't be allowed to stay the way it was." People talked about their passion, their commitment. Some talked about money, but people were divided, some feeling that pay should be on par with the private sector to attract talent, and others stating that this work is not about money, that the value is in the outcome, the helping, and a better world.

Personally, I went into nonprofit work because I felt that the world was and is a very unfair place and that perhaps through my work I could make it a little fairer. My values included benevolence and universalism, and also tradition, self-direction, and achievement. Whether because of the way my synapses are organized, my exposure to working-class values, or other life experience, I was driven. (Seriously, you don't complete a PhD without self-direction and achievement, neither do you become CEO or Executive Director (ED). Those things, and a serious masochistic streak.) And although they do not have to conflict, benevolence and universalism are in many ways quite counter to self-direction and achievement. If I get ahead, does that mean others are left behind? Am I perpetuating the class structure? How much should I make per year, given I work in a nonprofit that is supposed to use its resources for helping? How does that fit with my ideas of inequity and justice? In my choice of engaging in nonprofit work, I may be operating from universalism and benevolence, but just under the surface there may be other values that may not be as pleasing to the eye—or to my colleagues or to the mission.

I would venture to say that there are many components in the mix of why people go into mission-driven work. It gets very messy, wanting to help, to work for equality and social justice, wanting to make a difference in an individual's life or preserve a habitat, and the seemingly opposite ideas of being recognized for the work, getting paid (wanting to get paid, needing to get paid to pay the bills), the desire for a career. It leads to all kinds of internal dilemmas: am I a still good person if I want to "get ahead" in the nonprofit world? I want to see communities succeed in independent problem-solving, and at the same time I love it when people ask my opinion. Is it ok for me to want to be paid as much as a for-profit program manager given the people I'm working with are living below the poverty line?

Since I have struggled with each question, and I know others who have also struggled with the same ones and more, I'm using these as examples to demonstrate the need to recognize dilemmas, the dissonances within ourselves, as well as in the people we manage.

There is a primary, primal dilemma in nonprofits and nonprofit management: one's internal dissonances and the internal dissonances of others. Which are based in values and will result in behaviors in the workplace, and will lead people to agree or disagree on how the work should be done, which will then impact how people work with one another and how they do their jobs to get to the mission. I'd venture to say that if you have any of these dissonances and have not looked at them inside yourself, especially if you are in a management position, you will see the dissonances manifested in the behaviors of others, and they will drive you to distraction—which means distraction from your work and ultimately, the mission. Looking inside and acknowledging your own ideas, values, dissonances, and behaviors and their impact on others is the first step toward the development of organization-wide processes on understanding *how* the mission is reached. It's not easy, but it's necessary. You might want to make a list for yourself. What are the ideas, beliefs, and values driving you to do this work? Here, I'll make some space for you to jot some notes:

Jot your notes.

Ultimately in nonprofits, although we may agree on the mission, we bring different values to our work which will result in differing behaviors that impact us, our colleagues, and those who the organization is designed to serve. We might want to be transcendent, and we might also value hedonism. Or power. Or stimulation. Or tradition. And there's the rub: if we are in nonprofits and believe that we, as well as our colleagues, are operating solely from transcendence, then when someone asks for a raise we may be thrown for a loop. Or if someone is looking to move up the nonprofit ladder, we might look down on them—*this is not about YOU! It's about the mission—and we all agree on the mission*—but we don't all acknowledge what is driving each of us in the getting there.

If each of us believes we are operating from the same values, we are probably going to be baffled by the way some of our colleagues go about doing their jobs. A colleague who values security might not be open to new ideas, different ways of doing things. Another who values power might always be "managing up," so that their work is seen and recognized by those up the ladder. Someone who values self-direction may be seen as aloof, not a team player, and not contributing to discussions. Interpreting and acting on the value of benevolence can level a playing field through partnership creation, or it can maintain the us/them dyad if the staff person sees themselves as higher-up/better/smarter than those with whom they work.

By acknowledging all our values, or at least as many as we can think of right now, and how we prioritize those values, we may have a clearer understanding about the pathways we individually determine as successful ways to get to the mission. If we are not acknowledging our values, we are not being transparent to ourselves, and this can lead to a lot of confusion within organizations. Transparency and self-reflection are lifted up in the concept of Values-Based Leadership (VBL).

VBL has become a method and field of study, primarily focused on the for-profit sector. It is a process-based system that is grounded in the alignment of personal and organizational values; the mission is achieved through individual and corporate integrity, reflection, and authenticity, and there is an adherence to these values even though strategy or tactics may change (Saylor Foundation, 2013).

Different authors and researchers describe different principles—behaviors—that come from VBL, including self-reflection (establishing greater self-awareness for consistency in leadership), balance (the desire and ability to see situations from multiple sides to gain understanding), self-confidence (accepting yourself as you are with a recognition of one's strengths and weaknesses and a desire for improvement), humility (Kramer, 2011), and constructs of authenticity, ethics, and transformational leadership (Copeland, 2014).

The values that underlie the behaviors just listed fall under the broad categories of universality and benevolence and, drilling down to a second layer of values, include the worth of the human being, freedom of speech, learning, self-actualization, justice, and transparency. And the equality of women and men (and children, but not in the workplace, because children should be in school, not at the loom or in the mines).

VBL starts with being authentic, knowing one's self and being up front about it, which is very difficult because we most often don't want to look at, or deal with, our seemingly negative values and cognitive dissonances, and we *certainly* don't want to change behaviors—there is a belief that acknowledging "deficits" and the subsequent need for behavior change equates to weakness. Not so. Whining is weakness. Not addressing problems is weakness. Leading from behind is weakness. Examination and change in values and behavior, coming from a place of wanting to make sense of the dissonances, both internally and externally, struggling with the differences, is strength. It becomes a living demonstration of what is possible within a person and between people.

The authenticity that emerges from one's internal struggle can then be used as both a way to make decisions, and to "be," within a company/organization. A friend of mine talked about how authenticity factored into her decision-making in an organization where she was Director:

> not just authenticity about self, authenticity about leadership. For example when I was in the Executive Director role, the organization was going through a very traumatic change. It was a really controversial decision about the identity of the organization and I walked into a decision [to formally ally with several other organizations] that had been made four

years before I came in and that was still incredibly
controversial within the organization. The staff took
the leadership transition opportunity to reopen the
question, saying we actually don't agree with the
decision that was made, and we don't think it's the
right course to take. It was really hard. It wasn't the
hardest experience of my life but it's really up there
in the top five. And of course nothing was going
to make that experience an easy experience. It was
never going to be a pretty experience. But I think if I
were to walk into something else like that right now,
I think I would just be much more honest. I would
simply say I just don't know … And here's the thing,
[I'd say] "we can throw this whole thing open, and
together we can wrestle with all of this, and it's not
going to be pretty, in fact it's probably going to be
a huge mess. It's probably going to affect our work,
it's going to take an incredible amount of time,
things can get incredibly uncomfortable, because
the organization has already made commitments
to other organizations over these past four years,
and so ultimately if we decide that we are going to
walk away from those commitments it could fracture
relationships for years. But having said that, what
is authentic about this moment is we don't know.
You are saying you don't know if this was the right
decision, and that's important. And if you want to
struggle with it let's struggle with it, and let's make
this real, and part of being real means I don't know
where were going to end up. And neither do you."
If I walked into that same situation again, with the
same staff, that's what I would do and I would also
be brutally honest with the board. But if I were to
go into a situation like that again I would have that
conversation with the board before I ever took the
job. I would say this is what I need, so are you ready

for that? I think that would make a huge difference. In retrospect who knows? But my instinct tells me it would have made a difference.

She openly discusses the idea of struggling and of not knowing the outcome, as well as the possible consequences of working within the organization and possibly not having the time or capacity to honor the external commitments that had been made. She was self-reflective, had ethical concerns regarding the work getting done and the maintenance of relationships. She demonstrated humility and balance in her statement when she said that she didn't know where the discussion would end up, while pointing out that, if they were entering into the discussion openly, the team didn't know either. She had to ask herself many questions, including whether this organizational struggle would have genuinely been about getting to a structure/way of working that better reflected the mission, whether it was a way for people to maintain their own fiefdoms, or whether people just needed to air their concerns because this change was thrust upon them by the board (whom most nonprofit staff see as "outsiders"—sorry to be the one to break it to you, board members). Or one of a hundred other reasons. And then as Director, decide whether to open this up or not. And in retrospect, her decision would have been to open the discussion.

So although values are critically important and we in the nonprofit world probably agree on a lot, we do have differences that lead to different behaviors. People might be afraid to admit their values in nonprofits because they think they might be perceived as self-serving, lazy, arrogant, better-than. If you are worried—and by "worried" I mean these are things that are on your mind—about this, you are probably ok, you just need to do the internal work to determine if your self-perceptions are accurate. If you are *not* worried about these things, you should probably look for a job for which you are a better fit. The fact is that people in nonprofits are most often incredibly hard-working, putting in long hours and going above and beyond. Johnson and Lewis (2010) write,

> I am not sure that anyone believes me, but being president of a nonprofit requires as many hours as being a partner in a major law firm requires, and the work is just as hard.

Hard work can be in response to a person's commitment to the mission. Or it might be the case that people are working above and beyond so they don't have to look at their internal dissonances, like wanting to earn a salary that allows them to live comfortably when the people they are working with and for are starving or homeless. If we're not honest with ourselves, we'll never know. In nonprofits, it's especially tough given we are swimming in an ocean of values. The Pacific Ocean (because it's the biggest—that's how many values). Buffeted by different currents. With no life jacket. Not wanting to admit we are going down for the third time. Ok, so that's a little dramatic. But it can make for challenges.

* * *

When one is hiring to fill a position, how do we make clear the values within an organization so that people can know if they are a good fit? And conversely, how can we look at what people value and work to make the best possible hire for the organization?

One way to help both yourself, and those interviewing, know before a vacancy is filled is to clarify values within your organization. In this way, a leader or manager can develop a pretty good idea whether a person is a good fit for the organization, whether there is the potential for a person to become a good fit—whether their values and behaviors are aligned "enough," whether the way they act upon their values would better serve another organization/situation, or whether something within the organization needs to change so that the stated values are as valid for staff as they are for those served. As a manager, you can have a discussion of values as they relate to work (because otherwise you are meddling where you don't belong), and how values link to accomplishment of the mission—this is an "in-between space," the unexplored region between people and systems within organizations.

Chances are, if you are a manager, no one is going to come into your office and say, "I value power, and I want to have your job." But come to think of it, I *have* had at least two people say that exact thing to me during meetings ... sort of in jest—sort of. In those moments, I had multiple choices. I could be afraid that they were coveting my job, that they wanted to displace me and might act in ways that undermined my credibility to establish their own. I could have said, "well, I'm not going anywhere for a while, so you better start networking or get on Idealist or Indeed and look for something else." Or I could have asked if they *actually meant my job*—and laughed out loud because I was the boss and that was ridiculous. Maybe they thought I was not doing a good job. Or they were unhappy with their position. Or they needed to make more money because their oldest was accepted into college. Or a thousand other things. In these instances, the first thing I needed to do was to check myself, my internal state. Then from a place of genuine interest—or as much as I could muster at that point—ask them what it was about my job that appealed to them. Where did they see themselves in five years (in this situation it's ok to ask that question—in an interview, unless the person is just out of college, can we just ditch this)? What did they think they needed to move from where they are now to where they want to be?

By asking in a way that indicates you are actually looking for an honest answer, you have a better chance of getting an honest response, you are demonstrating your willingness to listen and that you value this kind of communication. And you have to be ready to hear what the person has to say even if you might not agree with it. And if you don't agree, you can ask questions to clarify, and if you still disagree, you can clearly, authentically, and, hopefully, helpfully state why you don't agree: you are not a limp noodle, and as a manager, this is your role.

Opening a values discussion between staff can be tricky because most people, unlike the ones who were forthright about wanting my job, are not going to talk about their individual values if it might make them seem a bad fit for the organization. And work is work, even though a person may hold values of altruism, universality, and so on, they are part of an organization to do a job and get paid. A way to get to values that underpin the work, and the behaviors associated with those values, is to establish a Statement of Values—an expression of what the people in an organization as well as those served have said they value, and a Code of Ethics—a statement of how values are put into practice (behaviors), for the organization. *Independent Sector* has great information on how to create both documents, what they should contain, and examples of each. These are, in essence, the underpinnings of "how" to do the work, which sit alongside the mission and vision.

CHECKLIST FOR DEVELOPING A STATEMENT OF VALUES AND CODE OF ETHICS FROM INDEPENDENT SECTOR

Independent Sector strongly recommends that all nonprofits and foundations develop a Statement of Values and Code of Ethics to help guide their policies, decision-making, and operations. Here is a checklist to help your organization begin the process.

Decide whom you think should be involved in the process. Be sure to include staff and the board. Other important stakeholders include major donors, volunteers, and program beneficiaries, each of whom will bring different and valuable perspectives.

Phase one: Focus your first efforts on developing a Statement of Values, which will later serve as the foundation for a Code of Ethics:

- Convene a group of stakeholders to develop a list of values that might be included in your organization's statement. Have the group brainstorm by answering these questions:

    1. What values are unique to our organization's mission?
    2. What values should every nonprofit organization and society in general uphold?
    3. What values should guide the operations of the organization and the personal conduct of staff, board, and volunteers?

- Draw from examples of values statements from other organizations as models.
- Develop consensus around the values that stakeholders believe are most important for your organization. Narrow these to the essential core values of the organization.
- Organize a small drafting committee to put the ideas into words. Reconvene key stakeholders to review and revise the statement as needed.
- Secure approval from the board of directors.

Phase two: Using the organization's Statement of Values as a foundation, now it's time to turn your attention to developing a Code of Ethics describing how you put those values into practice. Your resulting document will be a set of broad principles, not a detailed set of operational practices.

- Provide model codes from other organizations as a reference for the development of your own code.
- Convene a key group of stakeholders to decide on the essential elements that your code should cover, such as

    1. Personal and professional integrity
    2. Mission
    3. Governance
    4. Conflict of interest
    5. Legal compliance
    6. Responsible stewardship of resources and financial oversight
    7. Openness and disclosure
    8. Program evaluation
    9. Inclusiveness and diversity
    10. Integrity in fundraising and/or grantmaking (depending on the type of organization)
    11. Other areas of particular importance to your organization and field of interest

- Throughout the process, continually consult your Values Statement to ensure it is being reflected in the Code of Ethics.
- Organize a drafting team and have all key stakeholders review the draft to ensure support for it.
- Secure approval of the code by the board of directors.
- Design a system to ensure regular review of adherence to the code. Consider designating a board committee that will have oversight responsibility for compliance with the code.

(Independent Sector Values Statement and Code of Ethics, 2016)

(Reprinted with permission from Independent Sector. 2016. Checklist for Developing a Statement of Values and Code of Ethics. From webpage https://www.independentsector.org/ code_checklist.)

This is a lot of work, right? So not only do you have a small budget, stressed staff, and a vision/mission statement that may have taken a long time to create, you now have to go through more processes that take time away from the "actual work": program, fundraising, finance. An interviewee said,

> One of the drawbacks is that it takes longer. A lot of the times not everyone you work with is going to nec- essarily share that approach or that belief system, and times when you go about it that way it may prevent you from achieving results in the short-term. Trying to balance that is something a lot of people struggle with.

Inherent within the creation of values and ethics statements is the idea that values and ethics are important, that contrib- uting to the creation of values and ethics statements is part of the job, and that input and discussion/struggle are valued. Hopefully, this way of being carries over to all aspects of the organization, and to life outside work.

The secret benefit to undertaking this piece of work is that by doing this, you are engaging in a process which will pro- vide the experience of engaging in decision-making and work- ing together that can be a precedent for how work gets done in the future. It's like paving a dirt road—labor-intensive on the front end, but makes for a faster ride later on.

If, as is the case with many strategic plans, values and ethics statements are completed and sit on a shelf, the whole endeavor could end up being much less impactful than if they are printed and put up next to the vision and mission. Put them all over the office! In the hallways. In the bath- rooms (people always need reading material). If the outcomes from this process are taken seriously, if they are incorporated into the day-to-day functions and systems of the organization, if managers conduct themselves according to the Values Statement and Code of Ethics, and if people hold themselves and one another accountable, there will be a lot of effort at the front end of the process and less effort as agreed-upon ethics-based behaviors become part of the weave of organizational life; they will provide a guide on how to create systems that relate to one another, how interactions take place, what managing looks like. A lot of what was hidden can be uncovered. People in the organization will have a clear understanding—because they created it—about how and why the organization functions the way it does, and their role and responsibility to meet the mission in ethical ways.

A Values Statement and Code of Ethics can provide clarity and stability in a sometimes murky and unstable external environment. And, if the trajectory of the World Values Summary is correct, they can provide a roadmap to changing organizational culture from traditional versus secular-rational and survival versus self-expression; reiterating that people move from traditional (religious, respect for authority, obedience) to secular-rational (individual rights, inclusion, etc.) as their sense of existential security increases, and from survival to self-expression when their sense of individual agency increases (Inglehart and Welzel, 2005) (see Figure 3.2).

In doing this, we have built mechanisms for discussion and change within the organization, which is reflective of clarified values and is at the heart of *process*—the acknowledgment that things change, and it is ok, as long as it's not willy-nilly, ad-hoc, today-I-feel-like-doing-it-this-way change. But if our values can and do change and, subsequently, the behaviors associated with values change, what does this mean for our beautifully crafted values/mission statements?

Even though values can change, the values that form the foundation of most nonprofit work, like benevolence and universalism, and the drill-downs from those such as equality,

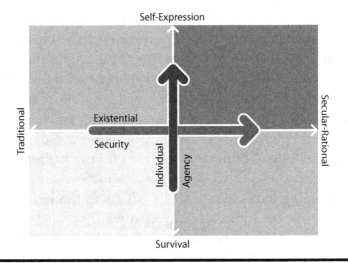

Figure 3.2 Possible trajectory of change in organizational culture based on changes in values and behaviors. (Based on text from Inglehart, Welzel, 2005).

justice, and compassion are the ones that probably will not change a great deal. There are others that may be added as an organization becomes larger, as more research is available, and as additional gaps or needs are identified. People within organizations need a way to determine common organizational values and ethics, and to establish methods on how to decide on changes in both. How an organization makes those decisions, including the variables of uncertainty and change, is the heart of process—its way of moving from confusion to clarity.

The International Rescue Committee (IRC), a nonprofit formed in the U.S. in 1933 (then called the International Relief Association [IRA], a branch of the European Relief Association), was created to help Germans suffering under Hitler, and later helped refugees from Italy and Spain (International Rescue Committee, 2016a). In its Statement of Values, the IRC includes compassion, commitment, solidarity, diversity, flexibility, efficiency, freedom and democratic ideals, opposition to oppression, collegiality, and proactivity (International Rescue Committee, 2016b). While most of these values are probably consistent with the values of the organization in 1933, I can imagine that the ideas associated with "proactivity" have changed or been introduced at a later stage in the organization's growth: At first, the IRC was helping people who needed to get out of Germany, Spain, and Italy because their lives were threatened by governments of the Axis powers. An immediate response was needed, and the IRC, then a much smaller organization, went to work; many people stayed alive because of the IRC's intervention. Today, through its programs and interventions, the IRC is looking at ways it can help mitigate the impact of disasters through linking development and humanitarian programs, decrease conflict through education, reintegrate former child soldiers, and participate in consortia and regional cooperation (Kastner, n.d.). Going back to Maslow, this time in an organizational sense, the IRC moved from Physiological/Safety to something higher—at least Esteem, that allows it to take a wider view of a situation to determine what else might be needed to help refugees, in this case by working to prevent or lessen refugee-producing situations.

The move from response to the inclusion of proactivity is a change in values. Although I am sure that IRC staff may have considered how to prevent or mitigate conflict/disasters, it did not seem to be a primary driving force early in the life of the organization. The values of compassion, commitment, solidarity, freedom and democratic ideals, and opposition to oppression have not changed; IRC still works with refugees and other displaced people, but by adding proactivity, the possibility of a whole new area of work has been opened. This is an example describing why process is needed, in this case to determine if the value of proactivity was one that should be included in the Values Statement, or whether proactivity is being driven by the opportunity for funding, a new partnership, or current thinking/research. Where did the idea come from? Who is going to make this decision? The board? People in the field? The CEO? Does this imply a change in mission? In branding (ever more important in the nonprofit world)? In the work at the country level? Is the organization prepared for this change—does it have the skills and expertise? Are there people who are committed to the original mission and not interested in moving from direct relief to the prevention of precipitating events? If the organization has values and ethics statements, and if those statements have been developed by the organization as a whole, there is a better chance that an inclusive decision-making process already exists, and many of the questions posed here can be answered within the construct of that established way of doing things—or process, if you will. Doing the heavy lifting up front makes discussions of this type part of the fabric of the organization, and it's much less scary to all because people know what to expect.

If we have clarified values and ethics, people themselves have begun to create the processes and boundaries within which they as individuals and the organization carry out its work. Because of the agreements reached, although I hope I am not living in Shangri-La (or Oz or name your perfect world of choice), people will feel more responsible to one another as well as to the organization, and will act accordingly; their behaviors will reflect the shared values and ethics in getting to the mission. Which leads us to relationships.

3.2 Relationships

Martin Buber, born in Austria in the late 1800s, was a philosopher who wrote about relationship. He proposed that we can interpret everything we perceive as outside ourselves as "other," and the "other" can be viewed as either "it" or "thou." If we use "it" to describe the other, the people and things in the world outside ourselves, then we think about the other as separate. Because of that separation, we use the other for itself or for the experience generated by it (Buber, 2000). I'm thinking about the computer here in front of me, the machine I am using to capture the ideas in my head and put them down in a form through which I can get them to you, the reader.

As an "it," I am the master of the computer (what a laugh—anyone who knows me knows what a joke that is), I control it, use it, it serves me. On the other hand, if we use "thou" to describe this computer (Buber extended "thou" to all things), it becomes not solely an object to be used, but an entity that I encounter, one that in that encounter can change the way I do the writing by allowing me to write almost as quickly as I can think, that might, through the color of the screen or the sound of the fan, trigger something in me that would not have been triggered without this encounter. I need to care for it if we are to continue to work together. I'm not sure what the computer gets from me other than maintenance and an occasional screen cleaning, but I'm hoping there's something good in the relationship for it, too.

Buber's essential thinking about the relationship between entities is that "all living is meeting," the idea that it is in the space between you and I that I can recognize you not as "the other" or "the it," as an object to be used, but without judgment as "thou," an authentic self/entity. It is here, between us, that something remarkable can happen, can be sparked. The act of living happens in between I and Thou.

In our organizations, depending on our structures, we meet people, systems, technology, and so on every day. Are we seeing them as it, or as thou?

You may look forward to going to work because you have great relationships. In fact, an article in the *Journal of Applied Psychology* (among other articles with the same findings) describes how frequent interaction with others, office friendships, and emotional support were strong predictors of job satisfaction—even more important than the nature of the work (Morgeson and Humphrey, 2006).* Or you may dread going to work because of relationships that … let's say … are more work than the work itself. And you're only being paid for one job.

---

* The study included, but was not limited to, staff of nonprofit organizations.

Although this is a section on relationships, I'm not going down Gossip Lane to the land of Unhappy Coworkers because this is a huge problem in organizations. And in life. It is so much easier to complain, to dismiss, to talk behind the backs of others. It avoids confrontation, minimizes hearing something you may not like, helps you feel superior, binds you to other complainers, helps you blow off steam. I'll say two things about this, and then we need to talk about how to build relationships that mirror the kind of world we want to see.

One: If you have a problem with a coworker, try to work it out. If you need some help in doing this, ask your manager. The caveat here is that your responsibility is to go in genuinely looking for understanding, and wanting to arrive at a way of being that works for both of you: "I-Thou". If you are being bullied, or sexually harassed, this is not the advice for you. You need to go to your manager immediately for help and to make a report with Human Resources (HR). The last thing we want is for a person who has been victimized to have to deal with their abuser alone, in work or in life. If it's not harassment and you've tried and still can't work it out, then you need to involve your supervisor and bump this up to the next level. If your problem is *with* your manager, again unless you are being abused or are afraid for your job, you can make an attempt to talk with that person. If your organization has created a Values Statement and Code of Ethics, hopefully "respectful exchange of ideas" made it into the "ethics" document. If talking with your supervisor does not work, you have the option of going to your manager's manager or to HR if your organization has a HR department.

Two: Intra-organizational relationship problems are often indicative of wider systems problems. As much as we might not want it to be this way, an organization often takes on characteristics of a family, with the "adults" (leadership and management, the higher-ups) at the top and the rest of the family (staff doing the hands-on work) lower down. In the 1960s, Murray Bowen developed the idea of family systems theory to help understand how families work so that problems could be resolved, with the goal of helping families to function more successfully.* Over time, the idea of family systems theory was applied to other structures, including companies and organizations, to help them solve problems. (Although there are parallels between family systems and organizational theories, at work we are all adults, and if the metaphor is carried too far, people are diminished, infantilized.) This is relevant to our discussion because sometimes systems, whether family or organization, are dysfunctional, and there are people within the system who become labeled as the "troublemaker" or the "scapegoat," those who are just incredibly frustrated by the problems they see/feel. Maybe the person in charge is deeply insecure and takes credit for all work, even when they didn't do it themselves. Maybe they are just angry all the time. Or completely inconsistent in their behaviors. Or narcissistic. This kind of dysfunction does not just "trickle down," it acts like a virus, infecting everything and everyone in its path. And if the person is in a leadership role long enough, the sickness becomes part of the organization's culture. Some people can disregard it, deal with it, and those who can't are "identified," potentially marked as "problematic employees"—or, as Buber would say, "Its." In a situation like this, relationships are not valued unless they reflect the leader's image back to that person. If you are in a workplace like this and you have tried to make change—that is, you have been identified as a troublemaker—my advice is to look for another job. ASAP. If you are a leader in an organization where people keep leaving, my advice to you is … actually, you don't care what my advice is because you see me and everyone around you as "It," so no more words for you.

* * *

* If you want to read more about this, go to The Bowen Center website at http://www.thebowencenter.org/theory/eight-concepts/societal-emotional-process/.

Now that we have a couple of the dilemmas taken care of, let's get back to relationship-building. One of the people interviewed summed up the importance of relationships at work:

> ... it's relationships at the end of the day that are gonna help to make management function. Relationship is communication, it's inclusive of communication, and if your management team isn't communicating with one another, it creates that dysfunction. If management doesn't have trust with each other, or trust in each other, it's dysfunctional.

Another contributed the following:

> There's one [idea about relationships] that I've been thinking on for some time and using it in different ways in various applications, and that is it basically works with the question that Drucker posed, who is the customer, what does the customer consider to be of value, how does one organize in such a way that that value is delivered? And I kind of boiled that down to the question that you can ask almost any organization, what's the benefit? You could also ask who benefits? The question for anybody I would ask, is "What's the benefit?" Once you know what the benefit is, and who the benefit is for, then one can begin to think about what kind of relationships do I need to have with the person or people benefiting, and what other benefits do I need to create or help create for people along the way? How does that benefit relate to the benefits of the workers, or the benefit of the producers, or the benefit of the managers, keeping in mind the mission embraces the benefit for some people, but he can overlook the benefits of the others who were involved. I wouldn't say that's the center of management, but it's a pretty

good way of integrating the phases of management by looking at what the benefit is, or what the benefits are along the way.

If you were going to have relationships inside your organization that reflected the world you want to see outside, what might those relationships look like? What would they be based on? Would the idea of relationship extend beyond person-to-person? How would people act toward one another? And how might you/your organization make changes to have relationships with those characteristics? Please take a couple of minutes to jot down some notes, and then we can continue the narrative (did you think I was going to do all the writing here?):

Relationships within my organization that reflect the world I want to see would look like:

Jot your notes.

What changes or methods can I/my organization make to have those relationships?

```
Jot your notes.



















```

In the world I would like to see, people interact respectfully with one another and with their environment. Diverse ideas and opinions are not shut down but are heard. Agreed-upon rules and laws apply equally to everyone. People admit when they are wrong and work to make amends. There is as much joy as possible generated in the space between I and Thou, because the core of the idea of process lives within those spaces—it's the way we treat one another and the opportunities we take to step back, pause, and reflect, that create the "how" of how we work. Yes, it is idealistic. My husband would say, "Lori, you and your rose-colored glasses." I'm ok with that.

Some things or methods that I and/or my organization might do to bring the living-as-meeting process to work relationships could include

- Space for open discussion (physical or "safe" space)
- A recycling can
- Hiring people who may look or think differently than I do
- Managing by walking around
- Organizational/team picnics (or whatever you all like)
- Office windows that open
- Purposeful, productive team and staff meetings
- Mutually agreed-upon values and ethics
- Processes for settling disagreements
- Clear job descriptions
- Equitable pay scales*

There are many that could be listed, and different people will probably have different ideas within their lists. It might be an interesting exercise for you to do with your team; however, if you have already agreed on a Values Statement and Code of Ethics, there have already been significant, and probably difficult, conversations that can lead directly to the development of I-Thou working relationships.

Relationships, whether personal or at work, *require* work; the success of those relationships, whether positive or negative, is an indication of your organization's credibility to those outside. Walking the walk. Building supportive, mission-reflective relationships at work is another form of process.

3.3 Trust

So this week here is our priorities, this what we expect to do. I don't like to micromanage I don't want to be like every three hours, "What are you

---

* People in the U.S. surveyed state that CEOs of companies should be paid no more than seven times the salary of an unskilled worker; in 2014, CEOs made over 300 times as much (Webbert, 2014).

doing?" I want to trust people. I want people to look at it and get it done, when we need that project, if they need help or have questions or want to raise a point that would affect things, I want people to take ownership of the work that they do and feel that it is their role, not just a task, it's being part of something. I think in terms of responsibility.

In nonprofits, we are in the business of relationships, and good relationships have trust as a foundation. Trust is a living thing, it is reciprocal and lives in between "I" and "Thou." Trust is an experience that leads people to feel safe or not to feel safe, to try new things, to do business as usual, or to leave a job. As a manager, you can tell someone what to do, or you can provide what they need to do their jobs, figure out whether you, as their boss, think they are ready to do certain things, and then let them go do it, while maintaining an open door in case questions or dilemmas arise. There is an element of uncertainty to this, it may seem like giving up control and giving responsibility to another person. And can be very scary if your trust has been abused in the past.

Trust is based on integrity, capacity, competence, and consistency and is created by being heard and respected, in the loop, included in decision-making, having those around you (and you) act with integrity, and providing support. Trust is shattered by inconsistency, bullying, not listening, hiding information, micromanaging, going back on commitments, not living up to your word.

A couple of caveats about work and trust:

1. Some people feel safer when there is someone telling them what to do, and if you are a hands-off manager, the perceived "absence" of structure can be interpreted as not paying attention, not caring, or a lack of guidance/ leadership. There is nothing wrong with someone who needs a structure-providing, hands-on manager. If you

are a manager or coworker, this is important to know so that the person can get their job done successfully or, if the department cannot respond to the work needs of that team member, a better fit can be (hopefully) found somewhere else in the organization.

2. As much as one might want to trust someone to do a job, I am not advocating for a manager to "trust" someone to do a job for which they are not qualified. This will most likely end badly, with results that may not be reparable and with a total loss of confidence for the person who was "trusted" to do the job. (Picture having an untrained person cut your hair. Or doing a hip replacement. Bad business all around.)

Trust deficits in organizations can stem from problems with leadership, as in the following example:

> I think that is a really deep-seated issue [in my organization] it's been like this for years, restructuring the last few years under [X] has caused distrust, lack of trust, deficit of trust, I think people have felt that they weren't listened to, they weren't part of the decision-making and again it's all about politics and egos, and decisions are made and they don't have any impact on the decisions that are made, but they are fully impacted by them ... Everybody is just a cog in this giant wheel right? And this is part of the lack of trust, which directly impacts the mission and how people are doing their jobs. People, again, don't trust that the organization is looking out for them. Because it's not. It's just not. And that's just how it is. It's fascinating. I mean it fascinating, in a really disturbing kind of way ... So you've got a lack of accountability and you've got all of the systems in place to force accountability because there's no trust.

No ability to input into strategic decision-making, restructuring as a solution to problems that have not been investigated, leading to excess accountability systems and negative impact to the mission. All due to lack of trust.

A second person described lack of trust as endemic to social justice organizations:

> This is kind of a deeper thing about social justice movements in general, again as part of this piece I was writing, I was reflecting on my own evolution, and I just grew up in a very racially alienated place. And I realize that what college gave me was a much more empowering racial narrative around my identity, and it gave me the ability to replace shame with righteous anger. The thing it didn't give me was, actually, love. And I find that missing from so much especially law-based social justice work, because law itself is such a language. I mean you say the word love in the legal context, and it's almost like you grew another head or something. So it's no surprise that organizations that are social justice organizations that are primarily using legal tools, that there is not a comfort level, or not a practice of bringing that sense of love into what we do, and really connecting with that as being just as important—just as important and more important than anger and moving the work forward. People who work in social justice nonprofits, they're so drained by stuff that goes on in the organization. And it's really sapping the energy that they have not just for their work, but for their life and their partners. And I also think that for us to just be at our best, all of these organizations that are working toward social change, we ultimately want a world that in which people can flourish, be at their best, and each of us needs that same thing, right? The thing that were hoping for, for the communities

that were working for, fighting for, I mean these are
the things, the exact same things. We need to be in
a place where we feel like there's trust. We need to
be in a place where we feel like we are heard and
seen for who we truly are. We need to be in a place
where we can actually get beyond those basic levels
of need, and be actualized, bring our gifts forward,
be challenged. Be creative like all those good things.

It's hard to trust when one is full of righteous anger. Even
if—as in the cases of killing unarmed men of color or people
who have been "disappeared" in political pogroms—the righteous anger is based in lived experience because the system
is so deeply unfair that it makes sense not to trust. Trusting
can get you jailed or killed. But what does this mean when
the lack of trust is brought into the workplace? People suspect
and expect the worst in and from others—including their colleagues. And there is probably an inherent distrust of authority, usually making managing or leading difficult. People may
be working toward the mission; however, the way they are
working may be fragmented and siloed and may be perpetuating an us/them (I-It) dynamic within an organization designed
to lessen the idea of us/them (I-It) in the world. Is it possible
to use the energy from the righteous anger to make change
outside the organization and at the same time develop a way
of working together internally that honors those doing the
work? I think it is possible; however, it would take incredible
self-awareness and perhaps a different way of working to get
to the mission.

In the Alternatives to Violence Project (AVP), a program
designed to deal with potentially violent situations in new
and creative ways, anger is described as an acknowledgment
that something needs to change. This is a great way to think
about anger as something both constructive and stemming
from a source that you might be able to do something about.
AVP provides ways of getting between the feeling of anger

and one's actions, to allow some breathing room. Anger can be a product of frustration, humiliation, and/or fear; the key is to get to what is at the root of the frustration/humiliation/fear and work on that, whether it is inside yourself or external. And to do it non-violently, because if we are always angry in the workplace, we may be recreating an environment where some people feel abused, less-than, humiliated, or afraid. And so the cycle continues. Not the world we want to see. Ask yourself what you are getting out of being angry—because I can tell you from personal experience that righteous anger feels *really* good. Puts you above things. Makes you special. And important. Fighting the good fight. Because you have a higher calling. And you are *right(eous)*.

In one of the interviews, a nonprofit leader talked about ways that technology and paperwork can undermine trust:

> I think if you spent less time doing paperwork or electronic work, you have the time to do the work itself. Being there doing that. I think that the kind of work that we are doing actually needs people, face to face, because regardless of everything, it's your relationships that you build, how you deal with people, the people-to-people thing, that really makes the change. That's how you build the trust, you don't build the trust through layers and layers of paper, through layers and layers and tiers and tiers of the organization, you don't build that trust. Because the more you have this, they become the bottlenecks.

Our electronic age leaves so much up to interpretation. I would bet that you have read emails or texts and are not sure about the intent or emotion behind them. Or you *are* sure and you find out later that you were wrong. And don't get *me* wrong, I am not proposing that we go back to letter writing and telephone calls and abandon electronic communication; Skype has been a wonderful interface, allowing people to build and maintain relationships with colleagues and friends in other countries, because people can actually see one another. It's amazing, like something from a sci-fi movie when I was a kid.

When I was directing international organizations, I would travel a great deal. My husband often would say, "Why can't you hold meetings virtually, via teleconference? It would be cheaper and you could stay home with me." And although this was so lovely because he really meant it, even to the time this book is being written technology does not afford the opportunity for exchange in the same way an in-person meeting allows. For anyone who has been on a conference call, or in a teleconference, the people "outside the room"—those connected by phone—can't hear, don't talk, can't tell when it's ok to break in, get a terrible echo, have to be on mute, forget they are on mute, and so on. Technology is great ... when it works. And it's just different when you meet someone/something face-to-face (or face-to-fish if you are part of an environmental organization; fish just aren't good with Skype). Trust can be built over Skype or phone, but being there, in person, is the fastest way to help build trust.

Another person talked about how trust in their organization changed over time:

> One of the things that I wanted to say about the ... organization that I haven't yet said, diplomatically ... when I joined the organization, I think that people from different parts of the world were treated almost similar. Regardless of your religion, regardless of your skin color, regardless of which country you came from. Things were almost the same. And I think that gradually what happened was that people from the north kind of ... the financial and development kind of a thing [took priority instead of] that everyone is equal, and human beings are equal, I don't think that that lives in the organization [anymore].

The largest humanitarian and development agencies work mainly in the global south, and are based mainly in the global north. High-paying jobs are held by people at headquarters, and in many organizations, decisions still flow from the top—albeit with some consultation with people on the ground. Given the power and wage differentials, it wouldn't be surprising if there were a lack of trust within an organization. Line workers in, and those being served by, nonprofit organizations may be skeptical. Or frustrated. Or angry. Or all three.*

Establishing trust within an organization does a number of things. It allows staff opportunities to grow, to discover, to feel a sense of self-efficacy, and to think critically and innovatively. It creates an atmosphere where people are not afraid to share their opinions and ideas, and are willing to listen to the ideas and opinions of others. It allows for a flow of information that lets people know the health of the organization, whether it is meeting its mission, and how it is working with other organizations. It allows staff to feel safe enough to do their jobs or to know what they need to do to do their jobs better. It allows for good working relationships. For managers, it allows them to do their jobs without constantly having to oversee staff and makes for a collaborative workplace.

How do you create trust? One of the interviewees described her experience:

> it was always like [I was a] third world woman and I had to always face that, and instead of being angry or annoyed, I realized that this was part of my job, and I had to face it, and if I was successful, I would pave the way for other women. So I took that on as another challenge, helping other women if I was

---

* To be fair, there are international humanitarian and development organizations that have moved to the global south, like CIVICUS and ActionAid, and others like Save the Children and the Norwegian Refugee Council that have decentralized.

able to succeed. I could open the doors for them, and people's ideas about women would change also if I was successful. So trust was built, because I am very extroverted, but I reflect a lot, it's when I would go back from work, and I would always say, what is the right decision? Not about ego or anything like that, and in my feedback, reviews, in my 360, this is the feedback that people would give me, the people I was supervising would always say, "She has no hidden agendas," even to the last, they would say "you are not at all political, and you look at that over there, and you think what is good for the institution. What is it that is our mission, what is it that will go over there. You make your judgement and you make decisions like that," and I think that people started to realize that I wasn't doing it for myself or for this little group or for that little group, you know it was like the vision and the mission of the organization was what was guiding me. It would take time but then they would start, then eventually the trust would start.

Apolitical. Transparent. Mission-driven. Reflective. Consistent. Role modeling behavior that others appreciated and, hopefully emulated in their work. When there was change or uncertainty, the associated fear was probably less due to the knowledge that things would not become personal, and, most likely, solutions would be arrived at through an inclusive process. Trust makes many things possible.

3.4 Uncertainty and Change

In addition to ideas, beliefs, values, and behaviors, and relationships and trust, there are two additional ideas implicit within "process": change and uncertainty, two things that can be incredibly exciting or incredibly frightening, or some mix of both. If we are going to equate or balance process with mission, and we've already dissected mission, we'll also need to look at change and uncertainty and what lies underneath.

Organizations, by their nature, like consistency. It is one reason that the continuity of succession planning in leadership positions is important. Funders like consistency and positive outcomes if an organization is to be funded again (to be fair, not all funders demand positive outcomes. Some are incredibly open to the learnings that come from failure, which can be very helpful to both organization and funder). *People* also like consistency. Just Google "Do people like change?" and you will get pages and pages of articles on why people *don't* like change; the resounding response is NO. It makes people uncomfortable. Frustrated. Afraid. Angry even. People may be afraid they will lose money, position, power, their home, their partner, their life. Who or what is supposed to change? How will change happen?

As much as organizations like consistency, in the nonprofit world, uncertainty is endemic. Uncertainty can be produced by: changes in staff; technology updates; passage of new compliance laws; the need for ongoing, up-to-the-minute social media presence; a new intervention; a more successful way of working; or funding streams. We may be uncertain because we might not be able to rigorously document impact or outcomes, leaving us not knowing if we have been successful. Rents are always going up, as are employee benefit costs. In some settings, the world political situation can change, putting staffs at risk. Staff members leave for other jobs, taking their knowledge and experience with them. Leaders, managers, and staffs can be willing to take risks or can be risk averse.

The Ellsberg paradox posits that people will opt to take a risk in a situation where they know the odds, even if they are quite low, and will be less likely to take a risk if the odds are unknown, even if the probability of winning is high (Ellsburg, 1961).

Hope can be grounded in as little as a 10-percent chance of winning, over an unknown chance, even if the unknown option is actually 99 percent. As humans, it is how most of us are built. Subsequent experiments have shown that there is a crossover effect between fear and hope, that when the probability of loss is less, people tend to be more afraid, and when the probability of loss is higher, people are more prone to hope. So if I am told that there is a 5-percent likelihood that my house will be hit by a tornado, I will probably be more afraid of this happening than if I was not given a risk percentage, and with that 5-percent chance, I would most likely hope that there would be no tornado damage. Or I could move to a less tornado-prone area.

But what does this mean for nonprofits?*

As examples of how uncertainty plays out, let's look at funding and ED turnover.

If an organization is well-funded and thriving, people don't need to hope. They might fear loss of funds and what that would mean (program and staff cuts). If the organization is in a precarious position, people might experience some fear, but there is a much greater reliance on hope that funds will come in.

For staff and funders of an organization with a respected, trustworthy ED, there wouldn't be a whole lot of reason to hope for someone else to come along. People might hope that the person stays, but according to the paradox, they will be more afraid of the person leaving. If the ED is not respected and trustworthy, I can imagine there being little fear of that person leaving, and a huge amount of hope that they will go. Far away.

Fear and hope—the children of uncertainty—leave a lot to chance (but you knew that). They can impel people toward extreme behaviors—frozen with fear or blissfully unconcerned, scrambling for resources or not actively seeking

---

* It means don't base your nonprofit in Tornado Alley.

them—that may or may not be helpful to the overall functioning of the organization. Probably not the world we want
to see, unless your world includes lots of adrenaline and/or
swinging in hammocks, which both might be good for holi-
days/vacations, but not so good for work.

There are managers who use change and uncertainty to
maintain power and control in an organization. If you keep
everyone guessing all the time, if people are always off-balance, you can think of yourself as the one who is holding it all
together, maintaining the organization. In reality, you are using
and hurting people for your own wacky ends. As a doctor (the
PhD kind) I prescribe therapy, a nice vacation, and that you
throw away your copies of *The Prince* and *The Art of War*.

If we are looking to minimize the extremes of fear and
hope within our organizations we need to, as much as possible, reduce uncertainty.* This does not mean we shun change,
we are not the Amish (no offense to the Amish, when the
end times come they are going to be the survivors); or that
we don't experience hope and fear; it means that these are
acknowledged and are balanced by known, consistent, inclusive, trustworthy processes and procedures. They are what can
make a significant difference.

3.5 Process: The System and the Act

"The how is really complex" (Interviewee, 2016)
    Ta Da! We are finally here at process.
    Two of the people interviewed talked about process in the
following ways; the first stated:

> I think a lot of times people become very mission-
> oriented, and that can become equated with if

---

* There are times when uncertainty can lead to breakthrough ideas; however,
  Louis Pasteur stated that "*chance favors only the prepared mind*," and who am I
  to argue?

you achieve the results, the means don't matter.
I happen to believe that's wrong. Means do matter. The mission is about having conversations,
and recognizing that everyone has something to
contribute, and getting people to talk about it. To
come together and work together to build something greater than any individual can. If we don't
operate ourselves that way, it's not only hypocriti-
cal, but also very counter-productive. Any results
we do achieve, anything we do accomplish, is
weaker because we didn't do it in the right way,
because we didn't live up to its ideals. So I think
that whether it's trying to attract donors, or trying
to work with partners, it's that you're okay with it
because it's what you have to do to try to get to
the next step. You have to take the time to work
through that. You don't want to just be about "mission accomplished." How you do it is about how it
grows and about sustainability ...

The second said:

Do you remember making a potholder when you
were a little girl? Where you've got all the different colors of those loopy things and in order for
the potholder to be something that you are actually going to give someone that is actually going
to hold together, you make that last little knot at
the top, that holds it together, it is the process that
supports the organization, not the product. It is
the process. It's not about [solely giving people
who are hungry] the turkey at Thanksgiving, it's
about that people are hungry now, we've identified a problem, let's build up from that, let's
brainstorm all of the issues, throwing them up
against the wall, let's prioritize to the best of our

ability, not mine not yours, the best of **our** ability
to determine what contributes to these issues that
we observe, then let's take constructive problem-
solving approaches and techniques to develop, to
the degree possible, discernible, measurable outcomes. If I'm asking you for money, I need to tell
you, and be able to prove what I'm doing. [This]
does not take too much time. It is not weakness
to use that approach, it is strength and it develops
a much stronger matrix, just like the potholder
because of all the warps and the weaves that have
to take place to come up with a coherent [object],
the product becomes the process, the product is
in the service, I was going to say the product is in
the service of the process.

Process can lead to growth, it can lead to completion, to
refinement. It can also lead to outcomes that differ from what
someone might want, and dissatisfaction if someone is wed-
ded to a specific intervention.

In the nonprofit world, we have a mission, the world we
want to see, and we need a way to get there. Going back to
science, in nonprofits, our hypotheses can be the interventions we apply to make change, hopefully based on a thor-
ough understanding of the cause of the problem. We think
that something is going to work, we give it a go, and, hopefully, we test to determine if what we have tried has made
change. The dilemma in nonprofits is that we are working with people, societies, and/or the environment: hugely
complex entities with a will of their own; with knowledge;
ways of doing things; their own processes. With their own
values, ethics, trust and relationship issues, uncertainty, and
ideas about change. Organizational mission expresses our
goal and, hopefully, we have wrestled with special/impor-
tant, higher-calling, directed-from-above paradigm and have

come out in a more authentic place—that wrestling is part of process.

Process is about *how* we move from confusion to understanding, what we include, and what we leave out. The idea of how, of process, has historically been focused on programmatic interventions, figuring out how we are going to get from problem to solution, unmet to met need, or from uncertainty to clarity—hopefully in consultation with the people whom the organization is designed to benefit. The idea of process as the way to get to the mission, as the program work, has been separated out from the workings of the organization, as if the organization were a train running on the parallel tracks of program and operations and the rails are connected by threads, going to the same destination but with little relation between the tracks other than a fast-moving machine atop them. Mission and process are the connectors, the (hopefully) seamless platform in between the rails (see Figure 3.3).

Process, as defined in this book, is essentially an agreed-upon understanding for staff and those outside the organization on how an organization will function, at all levels, to meet and as a reflection of the mission. It is a combination

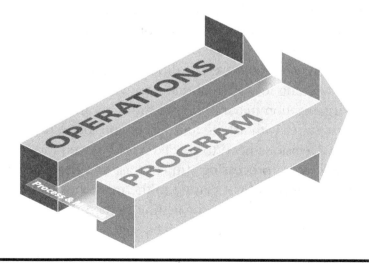

Figure 3.3 Linking program and operations in service of organizational process.

of values, ethics, trust, relationships, uncertainty, and change, and comes alive when it is linked to an end, the mission. It is the overall ethos for the way the organization, its staff including leadership, board, systems, policies, structures, and so on, conducts itself with everyone and everything both inside the organization and externally. It's a way to move from acknowledged or unacknowledged confusion, or difference, to understanding and cohesion. If process is created collectively and utilized by everyone, it becomes an end in itself, the living manifestation of the world we want to see. It's putting the train tracks back together, it is the organization becoming an organism, an entity, well expressed by an interviewee:

> People have to be able to participate in what it feels like so that as humans, as individual organisms, [they] can become part of the organizations that are organisms, that utilize and train our abilities to be creative collaborators.

How do you bring process from an idea to actions? Is there a "best process"? Organizations and people are in different stages of growth and development, and there is probably not one empirically proven process that works for all; if something is going to be processed or goes through processing, it is impacted by a force or forces that will cause change. Organizations are comprised of different people, with different cultures, working for different ends, so what process looks like in one organization may not be the same for another.

Process starts with asking and discussion, but it does not end there. Decisions need to be taken and moved forward; becoming lost in "processing" (in contrast to a process for decision-making) and not getting to the mission is as problematic as not having a process for getting to the mission, and is a recipe for misery. As one interviewee stated,

> See, there's process and there's solving the problem. And social work is really happy with the process.

It's what they do, it's needed in the world, and so process then can sometimes get in the way of finally making a decision and doing something. So you have process and then you have decision-making that comes out of process. I think a lot of the reasons management gets complicated is because people love process and they forget they're supposed to do something about the process and make a decision and actually solve the problem. And so we just process, and then we process and process and were talking about things now that we talked about five years ago. And we just process because, hey it's fun. And I don't know if that's because people are afraid to put their ass on the line and make a decision, because what if it's not right, what if it doesn't work, or if people just have some intrinsic aversion to making a decision. There's an accountability that goes with decision-making that does not go with process ... [people are afraid of] each other, failing, succeeding, my god what if you succeed? Now you really have a problem—I'm on this track oh my god we have to hire more people, we have to find more money, we have to do more of this and I think that most people are afraid of those things. So you put them in a structured setting, in which they would not organically come together, and that fear-based reality is just unconscious most of the time, but it's driving the process, so let's just stay with process.

How an organization gets to its mission is a lot about behaviors and, as we discussed previously, behaviors are based in beliefs and values, and people have a hard time changing. It is also about structures for decision-making, whether decisions need to be made about funding, program, policies, office space, pretty much anything unless the knowledge is so specialized, like the law, that people in the legal department will need to have final say (and there are times when difficult decisions need to be made and it may not be appropriate for anyone other than the manager/CEO/board to take that decision—more on this in the chapter on Managing). Allowing people to negotiate, together, how they will undertake work is a key to change; it allows for a person or group to live the experience of change. Revisiting a statement from one of the interviewees,

> If you lived all of your life in a one-step two-step environment, unless you have the experience of what it is like to really do critical thinking, to really take responsibility for your own behavior, as opposed to saying "I did what I was told to," there's no way to easily introduce organizations to another way.

Process is experiential, it is about making decisions, testing them to see if they work, reviewing and revising. It implies nuanced action:

> There are people that are committed to "on-off," and they cannot envision that there is another way. So how does the fact that there is another way come into existence? It's experiential. So much of human communication and other kinds of communication is nonverbal, something like 80 to 90 percent. If you lived all of your life in a one-step two-step environment, unless you have the experience of what it is like to really do critical thinking, to really take responsibility for your own behavior, as opposed to saying "I did what I was told to," there's no way to easily introduce organizations to another way.

Process is not a free-for-all. So where do you start? What do you ask? And then what do you do after asking? Having a transparent, inclusive methodology that people agree upon, is both part of process and key to a successful process experience (see Figure 3.4).

Figure 3.4 Harmonizing process (means) and mission (ends).

If you and your team/organization have created a Values Statement and Code of Ethics, you have already experienced a way of working together that has resulted in agreed-upon ideas. You've convened a group, brainstormed, been open to the ideas from other organizations, reached consensus, drafted, reviewed, rewritten, and finally agreed on your documents. You can use that experience of decision-making, as well as the values and ethics outcome documents, to move to the next step, determining how your organizational ethos or process will be reflective of the organizational mission, and how the mission will reflect the ideas of your process.

3.6 Mission as Process: Harmonizing Means and Ends

3.6.1 A Way to Harmonize Means and Ends

The following steps introduce one way to move from separate mission and process to a unified mission/process, resulting in a Process Statement. The way you get to the harmonization is part of process. Next, you will find one way to harmonize means and ends; how your organization will get to the process/mission link. The way you get to the harmonization is part of process. Implicit in agreed-upon understanding is that there is at least one way, a method, of getting to that understanding that includes dialogue, decision-making, implementation, and analysis. It's not so fundamentally different than the process you used for creation of the values and ethics documents.

There are things people will need to engage in discussions of this type. The mission statement, underlying ideas about how that mission produces the world one wants, information, history, a safe space and clear parameters for discussion, the knowledge that things can change and the ability to implement decisions, a way to determine if the decisions have been effective and opportunities to tweak or change the decisions for better outcomes. And a great facilitator. Really, really important so that the discussion can remain focused and decisions are made. In organizations, people who are good at facilitating, creating space for, and guiding discussion are often overlooked in favor of technical experts. Organizational structure is "boring" compared to program work. This is understandable, as the bills are paid by program funding. The dilemma is that if you have a staff of technical experts, the probability will arise that people will stick with their area of expertise, with how things should be done, and again, silos develop and consensus may be lacking. Ideally, having people who are able to do both, or to ensure that the organization hires people—even consultants—who are experts in the area of facilitation, structure, and relationships, is important, because people are then provided with a living example of how to hold constructive dialogues that result in agreed-upon and implementable decisions.

Organizational leadership will set the tone, so as a manager or leader, it is your responsibility to create an environment that mirrors a better world through making the space for this kind of discussion and work to occur. In doing this, you are establishing a culture within your organization. In his book, *It's Your Ship: Management Techniques from the Best Damn Ship in the Navy*, Captain Mike Abrashoff described his induction ceremony as commander of the USS *Benfold*. He was aboard ship as the new commander during the transfer of command ceremony and witnessed the ship's crew cheering when the preceding coercive commander left; he knew he had to do something differently, and he did. He listened to the crew and made change. He communicated all the time. And he was able to achieve excellent work from the crew after they were clear about the importance of the work (Abrashoff, 2002). If this can be done in the navy, it can be done in your organization.

3.6.1.1 Mission

Let's start with the existing mission of your organization. People in the organization may or may not know it, may or may not understand it. It may be in the operations manual or on a website or it may be displayed all over an office. About one-third of the people interviewed for this book could not remember the full mission statement of their organization. If people don't know the mission, starting with a staff review and preliminary discussion, getting ideas of what people think of the mission, what it actually means in practice, whether it is relevant, can be very helpful. You might want to break the mission into components and discuss each one. You can do this in a group, or you can start out individually by asking people to jot down their responses. If people have been asked to do this individually, take that data and compile it into a document for discussion; just make sure they know that their ideas will be shared.

Reviewing the mission in this way does not mandate changing the mission. Organizations will often consider a change in mission when a new CEO comes on board, if there are financial gaps, or if the organization is set on growth. One

of the people interviewed talked about reevaluating their organization's mission after a change in leadership:

> when I joined the organization, the mission was
> already decided and it was different than the one
> we're talking about now. With the current mission, it
> was a very participatory process, there was a lot of
> back-and-forth it took a long time but that's the mis-
> sion we came to.

The reasons listed in the previous paragraph can be appropriate catalysts for a change in mission; however, if the change
in mission is imposed by the board or the CEO without consultation, it can be organizational business as usual—no process, no inclusive decision-making. The idea is not necessarily
to change the mission, but to review the mission to determine
whether it reflects how the organization does all aspects of its
work to create a better world.

3.6.1.2 Structure and Functions

Structure within an organization is normally equated with
hierarchy, which by its definition is about relationships: how
do I, where I am, relate to you, where you are based on the
description (job, org chart, etc.) of where I am and you are so
that we can get the job done? It is a crucial part of process,
and is one of the main stumbling blocks, or obstacles, to integrating process and mission.

I am purposefully deciding to talk about structure instead
of hierarchy, because I think hierarchy implies a power differential (which exists, don't get me wrong, but we're working toward a more equitable world here ...) and structure
describes floors in a building, each supporting or being supported by others—above, below, or side by side. Uncoupling
structure and hierarchy is critical to managing as mission, and
in the next chapter I'll go into more depth on this. For now,

each level within the structure has a function and a relationship to all other levels or functions. One could also say that each function has a level, and that's why I've combined structure and function in this section.

Function is about *who* does *what* for *what* reasons, and how the who-what-what relate to one another. It is about what constructs/departments/clusters are needed to reach the mission and be in compliance.

What is valued in an organization will lead to the development or expansion of departments or groups as well as the hierarchy implicit in the system; this is often based on how the values of leadership (expressed or unexpressed) are weighted. If value is placed on raising public awareness of the organization, funding and hiring may be directed to a "celebrity wrangler," someone who knows how to access and then enlist famous people in support of the organization. Or the board may look to hire a well-known person as CEO. If an expanded organization is valued, emphasis might be placed on an increased fundraising staff including a private sector outreach department, or a merger with another nonprofit that has expertise in another thematic or geographic area.

In a formal organizational chart, Finance, Program, Human Resources, Development, and other departments may all be on the same "line," but informally the head of Program and the CEO may really get along well, or leadership may feel an affinity with Development and nonverbally prioritize that department. If people are paying attention at all, the pecking order is clear; no one has to say these things out loud, most of us are able to pick up the informal hierarchy from observation. And because it is informal and unspoken and creates those in-the-know and those outside, we have already created the world we don't want to see. Cliques form. People feel powerless and spiral down the drain of organizational misery. The mission is not accomplished in a way that is helping to create sustainable change. We may tolerate not-so-great behavior from a department head because we know that department holds a special place in the organization, and we are but meager peons in the org chart. We go to that person knowing that most likely, they will treat us—behave—in a certain way based on their values and beliefs and the informal role they occupy in the organization. If they are "favored" and unaware and ego-driven, the treatment might not be in the best service of the organization (or of one's hard work), and one might accept this treatment because we need a job, or we are committed to the cause, or we need to get something finished (or started). I'm sure you can think of additional situations.

The following are a few examples of the relationships between levels and functions in an organization:

- Person to themselves (including you)
- Staff to you as manager
- You to staff as manager
- Managers to other managers
- Staff to staff
- Staff to those served
- Those served to staff
- Staff to the work
- You to finance
- You to fundraising
- Finance to you
- Fundraising to you
- Staff to finance
- Finance to staff
- Staff to mission and vision
- You to external systems
- External systems to you
- External systems to external systems that impact staff/work/organization

There are many, many more that could be added.

You may be surprised at the first relationship in structure and function: You to Yourself. If you don't have a good relationship with yourself (or if you have TOO good a relationship with yourself), if you don't consider your impact on others, why you are doing this work, your values, and so on, there is a good chance you are going to manifest all of that uncertainty, ego, lack of clarity, and so on in your relationships with your team and others on staff. As one of my friends says,

> It may not matter what industry you're in, it may not matter what country you're in, it may not matter what the century is, there is something—I think human beings are flawed. [Our] consciousness does not afford a certain kind of perception that would get us out of this. And so we just keep repeating it all the time, and I'm not sure the industry really matters. I'm not convinced. I would be open to somebody trying to convince me.

You bring you with you everywhere you go. Maybe it's the biological drive to reproduce ourselves that pushes us to try to make the world over in our own image. Maybe it's fear. Whatever it is, when the pressure is on (or maybe all the time), *You* are going to "leak out" into your professional persona, no matter how solid that professional persona may be. If power is important to you, you might see levels as hierarchy, a ladder to climb. If you are an expert and that is important to you, you may want to spread your gospel, your way of doing things, throughout the organization and thereby see yourself as higher-up than the administrative staff. If you have been appointed CEO, you might believe you deserve the high post and that you have earned it by all of your hard work and effort, and you may think that those not as motivated and driven as you (everyone else) aren't as special, as important. You get the idea.

Your values and beliefs will manifest as behaviors along with everyone else's values, beliefs, and resulting behaviors, and the confusion and lack of clarity and possibility for skepticism, non-transparent ways of working, unhelpful power dynamics begin to look like a knotted necklace chain. Or Enron. Or a thousand other things that don't look like the world we want.

It's the spaces in between people and structures, in the meeting, where the intersection of the levels and functions happens, and it is in the interactions in the spaces in between that create or detract from an organization that looks like the world we want. If the relationships don't honor the "other," even in a "flat hierarchy," an organization runs the risk of recreating the top-down, power imbalanced, often poorly related structures we see around us.

The list of relationships in the previous passage is the starting point from which to ask the following questions: What are the levels/functions in my organization? How do they interact? Where are there bottlenecks? We'll pick this up again in Chapter V, "Linking Managing, Mission, and Process." For now, knowing how important relationships are, along with a deepened understanding of how the organization has currently agreed it will do its work and a clear methodology, provides the basis for getting to an understanding of the process/mission relationship.

3.6.1.3 Agreed-Upon Understanding

In most organizations, an agreed-upon understanding of how the organization gets to the mission consists of knowing the mission statement; knowledge of the group served by the organization, technical interventions to create impact, who to go to for program help, or to get reimbursed for your purchase of program supplies; and an idea of how the work gets done.

In many organizations, a discussion of the mission statement is about as far as people get regarding input into how the organization will move forward. However, as described earlier, there are a whole host of things that are not discussed, like values, ethics, trust, and relationships that are inherent in the mission, and the mission really only becomes alive when it is linked to these ideas.

Table 3.1   Gaining an Agreed-Upon Understanding of Mission and Process

	Mission Statement: Your organization's mission
Ethics	How is our mission statement operationalized through the lens of our Code of Ethics?
Values	How is our mission statement operationalized through the lens of our code of values statement?
Trust	How is trust operationalized in our mission statement?
Relationships	What kinds of relationships will get us to our mission?
Levels and Functions	What structure and functions does our organization need to successfully reflect the mission?

Breaking down the mission into how the organization would function if it were a reflection of the world we want takes the discussion further and can create an organizational culture. What would your mission mean if considered through the lenses of values, ethics, behaviors, trust, relationships, levels, and function? Would there be agreement? Would it stay the same, or would language need to be changed?

You can set up a table to help facilitate discussion with your team (see Table 3.1).

Oxfam, an international nonprofit headquartered in the UK, has the following mission: *To create lasting solutions to poverty, hunger, and social injustice.* Let's use that as an example* (Table 3.2).

I've used Oxfam as an example because they have really done their homework; they have values and ethics statements,

---

* Using Oxfam's mission statement in no way implicates Oxfam as part of this book or of participating in the development of this example.

Table 3.2   Example of Gaining an Agreed-Upon Understanding of Mission and Process

	Oxfam's Mission Statement: *To create lasting solutions to poverty, hunger, and social injustice.* (Oxfam, 2017)
Ethics	Statement: "exclude formal religious or political affiliations or other such affiliations which may compromise [Oxfam's] independence" (Oxfam 2017, p. 5) How is our mission statement operationalized through the lens of our code of ethics? Questions to discuss: Have you encountered situations like this in your work at Oxfam? How have they been handled in the past? What was successful? How have you said 'no' to a formal affiliation with a religious/political group? Etc.
Values	Statement: "demonstrate gender and cultural sensitivity in programing" (Oxfam 2017, p. 4) How is our mission statement operationalized through the lens of our values statement? Questions to discuss: How have you included gender sensitivity in your work? What were the results? Did they help end poverty or social injustice? Etc.
Trust	Statement: "Management of the Oxfam brand-risk is complex in that it applies to the highest standards of accountability, integrity, transparency and accountability..." (Oxfam 2017, p. 5) How is trust operationalized in our mission statement? Questions to discuss: Have accountability, integrity and transparency led to solutions to poverty, hunger and social injustice? How have you seen that happening? What are your core takeaways? Etc.

(Continued)

Table 3.2 (Continued)   Example of Gaining an Agreed-Upon Understanding of Mission and Process

	Oxfam's Mission Statement: *To create lasting solutions to poverty, hunger, and social injustice.* (Oxfam, 2017)
Relationships	Statement: "Affiliates will base their partnership on a relationship where they support partners to achieve partner aims; where partners themselves propose a direct way." (Oxfam 2017, p. 7) What kinds of relationships will get us to our mission? Questions to discuss: What kinds of relationships have worked best in supporting partners in achieving the mission? What obstacles have you encountered in relationships with partners that have impeded achievement of the mission? Etc.
Levels and Functions	Statement: "The constant search for better practice is developed as part of the organizational culture of the Affiliates and is facilitated in local organizations/ structures. This involves using and developing participatory processes and instruments at different levels: strategic renewal, planning, monitoring..." (Oxfam 2017, p. 8) What structure and functions does our organization need to successfully reflect the mission? Questions to discuss: How have strategic renewal processes within local organizations/ structures contributed to lasting solutions for poverty, hunger and social injustice? What would you continue to do? What would you do differently? Etc.

as well as a Code of Conduct and a Statement of Principles regarding how they work. They have put a lot of effort and time into answering the previous questions, as well as others. In their "Statement of Beliefs," they have specifically answered the question about relationships under the title of "Working Together":

> We are a confederation of affiliates, seeking maximum impact by building on our respective strengths. By working together, we enhance our collective

impact and cost effectiveness, and contribute to a just world without poverty. (Oxfam, 2016)

Oxfam creates lasting solutions through acknowledging and building on respective strengths and working collaboratively. This implies that there is respect between groups and individuals. It also indicates that people are aware of the strengths of others and a commitment to lifting up those strengths. If people are working together in this way, relationships have to include significant levels of transparency and responsibility that apply to all, mirroring a just world.

These kinds of discussions with staff can be both exciting and uncomfortable. They can impinge on "territories," can cause arguments between team members. But if these discussions are not had, how can we know that we are working internally to create the world we want to see externally? If questions are not being asked, if there are no opportunities to raise ideas and concerns, there will be a lack of understanding which leads to confusion and a reduced ability to meet the mission. People may believe things are being hidden from them. Their ideas and inputs will not be expressed, and they will be frustrated. Frustration leads to anger, and anger leads to loss of possibly excellent staff. Daniel Patrick Moynahan, former senator from New York, once said, "Stubborn opposition to proposals often has no other basis than the complaining question, 'Why wasn't I consulted?'" (Saxton, 2012).

Agreed-upon understanding is not having people agree because you have told them this is how it is; the operative term is "agreed-upon." The idea of opening up discussion and decision-making around the questions posed here and more can be scary; however, discussions like these do not mean everything in the organization is up for grabs: safety is critical, boundaries are important, and legalities have to be followed. If handled skillfully, answering the questions like the previous ones can build relationships and grow trust, as well as clarify how the organization meets its mission (through relationships and trust).

When issues are discussed, decisions are made and processes are developed by people inside and outside (those served) of the organization, there is a vetting of the overt and covert ideas and values that people bring to the mission, and there is the possibility to create a collective conceptualization of the culture and working methods, which can provide a new sense of clarity and ownership of both the mission and how the work is done.

3.6.1.4 Mission, Redux

After staff and those served by the staff of an organization have looked, in a transparent manner, at the mission, have agreed to a methodology for discussion, considered levels, functions, and relationships, and gained an agreed-upon understanding about what the mission implies, a second review of the mission should take place.

Does the mission reflect the new ideas, thinking, and methods that have arisen out of the discussions/decision-making/ implementation and assessment? You can't overthrow the mission entirely, but there may be ways of phrasing what exists to better reflect the ethos of the organization:

- We will work with children to advocate on their own behalves ... instead of ... we will advocate on behalf of children.
- We will partner with communities to uncover and uplift sustainable agricultural methods ... instead of ... we will provide the latest agricultural methods to rural farmers.
- Schools, including children, will create their own disaster preparedness plans ... instead of ... we will deliver disaster preparedness plans to school administrators.

You can see the difference—there is a recognition that individuals and communities served are capable, that their ideas and knowledge are worthy, and that they are participants in their own processes. There is no trickle-down here, there is equity and the recognition of the value of the other. It is a reflection of the integration of process and mission, linking means and ends as one.

3.6.5.1 Process Statement

At this point, you and your staff have worked through a review of the mission statement utilizing the method described, and have created a link between how the work is done and the goals of the mission. What is it within those discussions that has helped your team gain understanding? Was it good facilitation? Creating a safe space? Having background materials? Knowing what others were thinking? The specific things that helped you and your team get from confusion to understanding is your Process Statement.

The Process Statement should encompass both the intra- and extra-organizational processes of getting to the world you want. It could include some of the following:

Organization XYZ acknowledges that in order to create the world we want, how we get to the mission is as important as the mission itself. In that regard, we will

- Honor our Statement of Values and Code of Ethics
- Review the mission and this Process Statement every two years to ensure harmony and to take into account change
- Always view and work with those served by the organization through a strengths perspective lens
- Utilize an open discussion methodology when making organization-wide decisions
- Consider all staff as resources having strengths and not as "human capital"
- Ensure that all staff have the same understanding of the mission and process
- Trust that staff are working in the interest of the process/mission unless demonstrated as otherwise
- Be clear in job descriptions
- Listen to others

- Create opportunities for new functional or programmatic ideas
- Have open-door communication policies
- Create opportunities for staff from different departments to work together
- Provide information on resource allocation and program outcomes every six months
- More ...

If the methodology you used to get to this point (facilitators, small-group then large-group discussion, workshops, etc.) was helpful—and if you got to this point, it probably was—write it down. You will also have lessons learned, and some of those can be included in the Process Statement. You now have a clarified Mission Statement, a Values Statement, a Code of Ethics, a Process Statement, and a Decision-Making Methodology. You can name this packet whatever you want, the "How We Do Things" packet or the "This Was a Lot of Work" collection. Gaining this clarity, how you will do the work, is critical for our later discussions on managing and, if you are able to get to this point, determining managing as mission will be much easier. In fact, you'll have lots of insights to bring!

3.7 Outcomes of Process

This has been a very long discussion of process complete with charts, some lists, and many, many ideas. If staff have talked through values and ethics and have had a hand in decision-making through a transparent methodology, there is a better chance that they will interact in ways that mirror the change the organization was created to achieve; the spaces between people, teams, and systems will be better understood; and your internal organizational interactions can be the same as those we want to see externally. If staff have had input into what is valued and how those values are implemented in

relation to the mission, it is going to be much easier to determine what is actually needed in the organization in contrast
to what may be vanity- or ego-driven. And the possibility for
people/teams/systems to work well together is heightened,
because everyone is pushing in the same direction. If problems arise, a precedent for how the organization will solve the
problem through discussion, decision-making, implementation,
and assessment has been set. Process. Progress. Mission being
accomplished.

Ah, but what about the dilemmas within process itself?
You may think to yourself, "It's not as simple as is written in
the previous sections! So much time! So much effort! So much
potential for disagreement!" So let's look at a few examples
and ways to deal with the dilemmas.

3.8 Dilemmas within Process

Like most other concepts in this book, process is fraught with
fear, hope, unmet expectations, conscious or unconscious values and behaviors. During interviews and in my experience, the
following are issues that are cited as dilemmas in process:

- It takes too long.
- We don't have enough time or resources.
- We need to focus on the work itself.
- People will present wacky ideas that are not helpful.
- It takes too long.
- The staff will become divided.
- We already know how to do the work.
- We'll never get agreement.
- It can move beyond work and into personal beliefs and
  that's against the law.
- How can human resources people meaningfully input
  into financial systems?

■ How can finance people meaningfully input into human resource procedures?
  – Why would either *want* to input?
■ People won't say what they really think.
■ There will be conflict.
■ It takes too long.
■ I will lose control of the organization.

I am not going to go through all of the (real or imagined) dilemmas listed here, because that is a book in itself. I'll discuss three that have implications for others on the list and, using whatever methods work for you, you will be able to figure the others out—you've come this far, and I have great faith in you.

3.8.1 Losing Control

Let's start with the last one first. If you open things up for discussion, it's true, you might lose control of the organization. It might fly apart in all directions, people may end up hating each other, you may not be able to reach agreement, and you may lose your job. All possible and, at first, if no discussion of this type has happened before, you may experience some variations of these events. Having small group or individual discussions prior to a large-group discussion can be helpful. If you keep the discussions focused on the mission, on the work, and you authentically want to work through the dilemmas, that will show, and my experience is that people will follow your example. It also provides the opportunity for you to learn a lot about your staff, who is committed to the mission, who is in it for the amazing salary, who genuinely wants to be part of the team, and so on. And the truth is that if you need to control your organization by threat of having people fired—although sometimes helping someone move on to another organization is a good idea—in truth you have created a totalitarian regime, and you should be ashamed of yourself.

You are always going to have people who need to be in opposition to any system or structure that is in place. We are in the business of righting wrongs, fighting inequality, ensuring human and environmental rights. For many of us, this is part of the fabric of who we are. However, if a person is so deeply opposed to levels and systems, it might be a good idea for them to think about work outside organizations. If you have open discussions, that person's behavior and inputs (or lack of inputs) will rapidly make their orientation known, and the group, along with your managerial leadership, will set the parameters for the how of the work. The person either will decide to change, will look for another job, or may be terminated.

Counterintuitively, inclusion in determining the *how* of the work, leading with a light touch, and allowing people to do their jobs within a system they have had part of developing will allow people to come to you with problems so that you can solve them together. The transparency and authenticity—and an open door—that you demonstrate allows for a safe space that actually gives you an ability to meet the mission and develop staff who can think critically. The micro and macro become the same. The process and the mission are then one. Win-Win.

3.8.2 Wacky Ideas

People will present wacky ideas that are not helpful. Really? Who have you hired? If you were captain of a North Sea crab boat like on the TV show *Deadliest Catch* and you hired a person who hated the cold, was afraid of large spider-like crabs, had horrible motion sickness and claustrophobia, and couldn't stand the smell of fish, unless the person had a profound reason to sign on to the crew and overcame all these issues, you probably wouldn't bring home the bacon ... sorry, the crabs … ok, you would not *get to the mission*. You know what I mean. The same is true for nonprofits. People know the mission and most likely have some experience or deep interest in the work that is being done. There are many interview questions you can ask that get to someone's behaviors which gives a glimpse of their values—in fact, there are many, many tests that new staff can take to determine if their values and priorities will fit with an organization. So the chance of someone going way, way outside the crab trap is small.

The real dilemmas emerge when people introduce new ideas or want things to change within an existing system or structure and, for whatever reason, that system/structure is resistant to change.

This had been particularly true through the latter part of last century as shown by research in the private sector; CEOs by and large wanted to preserve the status quo, making innovation difficult (Anderson, 2004). More recently, a PricewaterhouseCoopers study found that 61 percent of private sector CEOs consider innovation either their utmost priority or one of the top organizational priorities (Percival and Shelton, 2013). The private sector *wants* wacky ideas—as long as those wacky ideas make money. And since we have already determined that we are not about making money as our mission, perhaps we need some combination of stability and "disruption"—although I detest that word and all forms of jargon that create dyads in our thinking. Like countering victim with "resilience." Or capacity-building instead of training. I will be the first one to say that language is really, really important and can make change. I realize it's helpful to shift thinking, but I just can't stand the bandwagon aspect of it. *That* is going to be an unpopular idea … now where was I? …

Yes, let's say that it would be helpful to have stability *and* innovation. We need to be open to new ideas, new ways of doing things, not afraid of them, while not throwing out what we know works. The mission is the starting point. People can rally around the mission and share and prioritize the values and behaviors they feel relate to the mission and a better world. And then everyone who is participating has a framework within which to operate. They know the rules because they have made them, and so they are probably not going to suggest that a substance-abuse treatment program utilizes a large-scale crabbing intervention as part of their program.

3.8.3 Time

> Decision-making to the highest degree possible
> should be collaborative in nature, knowing that it
> takes more time. (Nonprofit leader)

All of this discussion and decision-making, looking at values and ethics, doing the prep work of reading documents and thinking about them, takes too long. Uses too many resources. We have to do the **work**, we don't have time to talk about all these things. Our donors will be unhappy because they may not see direct change, it's much harder to measure. There can be consequences to focusing on allowing people to present new ideas, to coming to agreement on all the things we've already talked about.

Remember the interviewee who was hired into an organization that had recently undergone a board-created structural change? She talked about the impact of the board not consulting the staff and the idea of taking time:

> And here's the thing, we can throw this whole thing
> open … we can wrestle with all of this, and it's not
> going to be pretty, in fact it's probably going to be a
> huge mess. It's probably going to affect our work, it's
> going to take an incredible amount of time, things can
> get incredibly uncomfortable, because the organization
> has already made commitments to other organiza-
> tions over these past four years, and so ultimately if
> we decide that we are going to walk away from this
> it could be deeply uncomfortable, and could fracture

relationships for years. But having said that what is authentic about this moment is we don't know. You are saying you don't know if this was the right decision, and that's important. And if you want to struggle with it, let's struggle with it, and let's make this real, and by real part of being real means I don't know where were going to end up. And neither do you.

Struggle. Discomfort. Not meeting obligations. Fractured relationships. A lot of time. The uncertainty of not knowing where things will come out. All realistic concerns. All reasons for not opening discussion and, given particular situations, these reasons can be appropriate. But not discussing because you don't want to feel uncomfortable is not acceptable.

Another person talked about things taking time:

> One of the drawbacks is that it takes longer. A lot of the times not everyone you work with is going to necessarily share that approach or that belief system, and times when you go about it that way it may prevent you from achieving results in the short-term. Trying to balance that is something a lot of people struggle with. Another drawback is that a lot of people, a lot of your partners, donors, may not see you doing much, even if you are. It's very hard to put in a donor report that we've had this many conversations that helped evolve us from these two different viewpoints to this one. It's like, that's not really doing anything, that's what a lot of people would think, but it is doing something. I think one of the drawbacks is that it's very difficult to paint a concrete picture. I always talk about development in a way that it's not that development is achieving anything, it's the actual work. Getting up to a certain standard of living is not development. Development is how you continue to make progress, and it's hard

to explain that because people want to know if you've done X number vaccinations, the number of books you've distributed. But it doesn't matter if the kids aren't actually going to school and using those books. [...] It puts you in a difficult spot in terms of perception, so that's a drawback, but I think if you find the right people you can do the job right.

The idea that development, whether community, national, or international, is *not an end product but an ongoing process* achieved through working together, building relationships, and ongoing change is an excellent example of process as mission, and turns the idea of things taking time on its head. If the process is the product and the product is the process, we need to reimagine what "taking time" means. This idea was reinforced by another person who said that *change, really long-term sustainable change, comes from change and development within communities.*

As humans, we are fundamentally incremental beings in a world of information superhighways, bullet trains, fast food, instant communications. An interviewee said,

If this thing doesn't work, you try something else. It's hard. I think people don't change easily because I think it requires a lot of perseverance. And so we are living in an instantaneous world. For God sakes if I read one more person tweeting something, I'm gonna puke. You cannot communicate something in whatever amount of characters that is. So to actually create something substantial, something meaningful with roots, requires doing the opposing action of the direction that society is moving in.

Organizations want stability, and the world is demanding change. All the more reason to be clear about how we get to the mission, because if we are always working to catch up, if we are piecemeal putting together messaging and are not on the same page regarding how we do the work, we are wasting time. Work needs to be redone, information is not communicated, and we are less effective.

Process, at least in the beginning, takes time. Process discussions can start as discreet pieces of work, like the creation of a Values Statement and Code of Ethics and, with time, how things are done, including changing how things are done, becomes second nature and becomes an integral part of the work and organizational culture. We have to be ok with some things taking time. We actually have to embrace it, swimming against the tide of the instant solution. Otherwise, we are leaving a whole lot of people behind and reinforcing a world of duality and non-inclusion with exponential speed.

3.8.4 Other Outcomes

I wanted to write "good" outcomes, but I've made myself so aware of dyads that I just can't think of a word that does not contrast with "dilemma." Even dilemma is jargon. It's a way to imply that things are not "bad," but that they are "of concern" or "need review" or _____ (fill in the blank with your word of choice—I'm exhausted).

Process provides an opportunity for examination; not navel-gazing, but the opportunity to turn on the lights in a room that was dark or dimly lit. It gives us the opportunity to test ideas. To understand others. To listen and to be heard. To look at the spaces in between people, departments, roles, levels, at how they interact within the organization and how the organization interacts with those served and external groups. An opportunity to be clear about how the nonprofit functions, its values, ethics, and methodologies, and to make that clear to others.

At best, process allows us to examine our own values, ethics, and behaviors to determine whether the organization is a good fit for us, whether nonprofit work is a good fit, or whether we might be better off in another job or sector. THERE IS NOTHING WRONG WITH THIS. In fact, it is wonderful! If there is a situation with a better fit for you, I am thrilled! I encourage you to pursue your goals in a place where your values and goals are more aligned with your new organization/company. By doing this you will be happier, and you will make the lives of your team members, your supervisor, and especially those served by the organization much better.

In addition to examination/reflection, process is the cornerstone of an organization's credibility. As an interviewee said,

> Our mission is about getting people to come together working for a common good, everyone's voice is heard. If you manage your team in a way that suppresses their voices, you're under cutting your mission. This is why the how matters. Because you want to be able to be sure that you are living the values that you aspire to. And those that you are espousing to everyone else. It's more than personally how people view you, it goes to your credibility professionally. I can't go into a room to talk with a partner to talk about how we need to find their agency and voice within the work if I go back to my office and I'm like, "Hey, you need to do that, you need to get me that now." You can't do that because the partner is going to [see] that [in] your email trails and everything like that, people are going to find out. "You're not living up to that, not doing that, why should I as a partner trust you to follow through on the work?"

If you think that the people around you or those with whom you are working don't know whether you are being authentic or not, you are kidding yourself. You are the emperor without clothes. Your coworkers know if you are credible. Do you accept responsibility? Do you live up to your commitments? Are you honest? Do you say one thing and do another? All indicators of credibility.

In nonprofits, we are often working with people who have been through incredibly difficult life experiences and have had to constantly read their environment just to survive. Safety is a prerequisite for any type of nonprofit work, particularly if you are working with people. We know that hypervigilance is a by-product of experiencing traumatic events. In an emergency, people are running from something harmful and toward something they are hoping is safer. People are attuned to behaviors, actions, words, inflections that let them know if they are safe or not, and one of the big factors in safety is whether the person who is in front of them is credible.

Human rights are the international baseline for credibility. If an organizational value is "guaranteeing the rights of all human beings," as nonprofits, we need to mirror that within the organization. If not, if our leaders are not ensuring the rights of staff, and if staff are not treating other staff respectfully as per Article 18 of the Universal Declaration of Human Rights, which states *Everyone has the right to freedom of thought, conscience and religion*, it will be much more likely that staff will have similar attitudes and/or behaviors regarding the people or the cause the organization has been created to serve.

Another outcome of process is that everyone in the organization is on the same page, because they have written the book. There is clarity around mission and how to get there, as well as when success is achieved, and there is a way to go about changing things that are not working. Staff have created the culture; they have experienced a way of working together that has changed them, and they are torchbearers for a different way of thinking about and doing work, of getting to the mission.

People can then also know if the mission has been met and whether the organization is still needed—this is a huge issue and problem with nonprofits; in companies, if there is no profit the business ends. In nonprofits, if there is no money, the organization closes shop. But because things like relationships and ensuring people have jobs "get in the way" in situations where people actually care about others, there are times when nonprofits go on longer than they should. Closing, whether the mission has been met or not, should never be a surprise; if there is participation and transparency, allow people to be involved in this kind of decision-making and allow them time to look for new jobs if shutting down is the choice.

As you probably know by now, I am not a proponent of structural change as a substitute for addressing the confounding issues within a nonprofit: restructuring is often used as a fast way to avoid addressing underlying problems. Avoidance is like denial and, although it works to an extent as a defense mechanism, it ultimately results in the recreation of problems because the underlying issues have not been addressed. As a manager, it is your job to work with your team or wider staff to develop process that gets at the etiology of problems and creates modalities through which problems can be solved.

And on that note, let's look at managing.

Chapter IV

Managing

Everyone things of changing humanity, but no one thinks of changing himself.

Leo Tolstoy

1900

So much of what we call management consists of making it difficult for people to work.

Peter Drucker

n.d.*

Management. Managing. Manager. Manage. Four forms of the same word, most likely traced to the Latin "*manus,*" or "hand." In Italian, their origin is "*maneggiare,*" meaning "to control," as in training horses (Harper, 2016; *Oxford English Dictionary,* 2016). I think a horse in the hand is worth … no wait, that's bird in the hand. Horses weigh too much for one hand.

---

* This quote is attributed to Peter Drucker. Staff at The Drucker Institute could not find a source but stated, "It sounds like something Peter Drucker would have said."

If one has ever worked with horses, you know that they are very large animals. They have big teeth and hard hooves, and some of them have an iron will. Anyone who has been on a trail ride knows that a trail horse is absolutely clear about the shortest route between where it is at any given moment and the barn, where it can divest itself of you and maybe get something to eat. *Their* goal is to rest and eat and hang out with the herd, and *your* goal is a trail ride—for which you have probably paid a lot of money—and those two ideas can conflict. There's not a lot of talking things out, so taking the reins in hand and directing your mount back onto the trail after he has decided to graze on some grass next to the road can make you happy, and the horse, well, he can comply or throw you but it's a lot of effort to buck you off, so moving on seems to be your mount's likeliest choice ... Hold your horses, Lori! Get back to the subject at hand.

4.1 Defining Management

The word management and its derivatives are noun and verb, a "person/thing," (manager/management), an action (managing). "Management" can be experienced as something separate and apart from the actual work being done, as in, "We are labor and they are management," or "The powers that be—management—have decided to change our health insurance plan," or "Management is merging our organization and another organization." Seen as something monolithic, separate, and in control, management can be perceived as an entity that non-managers have little control over, an entity that imposes rules and methods and timecards and meetings and whether we stay employed or not. It was and still is a central reason for unionization. The idea of management as something separate and apart from the "real work" always makes me think of Kafka and his idea that bureaucracy becomes an entity in itself and is destined to quash individuality and creative thought.

A manager is often the person who conveys messages and policies to workers, and who is responsible for seeing that the work gets done. For many of us, management (the structures) and managing (the act) are viewed as external to our day-to-day, unless we need something like sign-off on an expense report or are reporting on results. Or maybe you've had a success and your manager calls you in to congratulate you—which is great and as it should be in the world we want to see.

Managing is the way a person undertakes their role as manager within the bigger structure of management. It is the active part of management, and is the centerpiece of managing as mission. It's important to understand the nature of the words because management was, and in some cases still is, a value-laden dividing line in the workplace.

In companies or organizations, management—as in the act of managing—has been, and often still is, the organization and coordination of activities in order to achieve defined objectives. Those activities have been categorized as forecasting, organizing, planning, commanding, coordinating, controlling, and directing an organization's resources (*Business Dictionary*, 2016). Management systems are formally defined as the framework of policies, processes, and procedures used to ensure that an organization can fulfill all tasks required to meet the mission (FitSM, 2016), and managers are seen to have the power and responsibility for decision-making to ensure this takes place (*Business Dictionary*, 2016).

Management structures are the overarching ways the company or organization is, well, organized; this can be found illustrated in an organizational chart.

This rest of this chapter will consider traditional management styles and functions, teasing out differences between structure and hierarchy relating to management. It will then move to the act of managing, which includes two important elements that are not often considered in traditional definitions: relationships and people, although this is changing in both management literature and practice. We then consider the role of individual change in successful managing, and finally, we will ask the question: Do you *want* to manage?

I would go back to the World Values Survey and propose that we are in lightly charted waters in organizations and companies; we have many years of codified ways to run companies and organizations rooted in traditional and survival modalities, and we are now moving to a secular-rational and self-expressive culture. There is less respect for, and subsequently a questioning of, authority, which probably leads to less obedience, and a greater desire for self-expression based on a sense of increased individual agency. Increased levels of education also contribute to this, as does technology (Saxton, 2012), and voila! We have millennials. This is not a—wait for it—*value* judgment or a commentary on millennials, in fact I would say that millennials are the face of this change, and they take a lot of the flak because they are the embodiment of the move to secular-rational/self-expressive modalities. I'm putting forth that this change it is one explanation for the explosion of books on management (and leadership). We are creating new charts, new guides. Peter Drucker writes that "With the rise of the knowledge worker, one does not 'manage' people, the task is to lead people. And the goal is to make productive the specific strengths and knowledge of every individual" (*Wall Street Journal*, 2009). Much has changed over the past 50+ years, from a strictly top-down, command-and-control model to a more participatory way of working including open decision-making, sharing of ideas, strength of teams.*

Also not a value judgment (coming on the heels of quoting Peter Drucker) is the lack of women's voices in the historical and current literature on management: It is a fact. As part of the background research for this book, I did an internet search for "books

---

* Management systems have evolved over centuries; if you would like a good synthesis of the evolution, you can check out http://faculty.wwu.edu/dunnc3/ rprnts.historyofmanagementthought.pdf which describes management schools of thought as well as provides additional references.

on leadership and management." A survey of three of the top five non-promoted sites to come up, *Inc.*'s Top 50 Management and Leadership Experts (Hayden, 2014), *Top Management Degrees'* (2016) Top 50 Bestselling Management Books of All Time, and *Time*'s (2016) The 25 Most Influential Management Books, provided the names and works of 125 authors and experts, and five were women. Cinco. Cinque. Fünf. Not to expose my feminist leanings—but I will—no wonder women are making less than men and why we have so many problems with management. At least half the population has had little voice in the creation of the structure/systems/policies/processes/procedures that have been associated with managing.

If we are going to successfully manage to get to the mission, and to ultimately manage **as** mission, we need to assess the dilemmas—as in confusion about what we actually mean by management/managing, our reactions to the term(s), societal change, and ideas and guides in books written almost exclusively by men—before we generate solutions. As a non-profit leader said, "unless you have [know] what the sickness is, the diagnosis, then the operation cannot be successful. The patient will not be cured so it's the same in the social. It's a natural law so to speak. Unless you can talk about the problem and find out what the problem really is, how can people find out the problem when ideas, thinking, viewpoints are controlled? Solutions we still have not found because so many people are in situations of managing or being managed that take so much energy, the mission is impacted."

4.2 Management: Styles and a Couple of Dilemmas to Get Us Started

There are lists and lists of management "styles"; books have been written describing them, lifting up the idea that management is synonymous with an individual person (the manager) or an organizational culture (management). Styles include Directive,

Authoritative, Affiliative, Participative, Pacesetting, Coaching, Persuasive, Democratic, Chaotic, Laissez Faire, Management by walking around, Paternalistic (Cardinal, 2015).

There are "how tos" for managers, guides and templates for running better meetings, creating agendas, and resolving conflict. Management can be accomplished in 14 steps, 10 steps, 32 ways of doing it right, 6 tips, 1 minute, 5 disciplines. There are a thousand articles and journals. So much research exists! So many books and blogs and websites. Consulting businesses. There are so many questions. Is a manager a leader? Is a leader a manager? Does management create organizational structure/systems/policies/functions or do the structure/systems/policies/functions dictate management styles—or are they so enmeshed that they can't be teased out? Do we need managers? People interviewed for this book said,

> I think management, a lot of times, is being able to coordinate everyone's contributions to ensure that you're moving towards a common vision, that you are succeeding, and achieving your mission. I think it's important to differentiate between operational management and program management, because a lot of times people, when they're talking [management they are talking] about operational management or talking about balancing the budget. That's a role in management, it's an important one, you want to make sure you have resources. I think equally, in project management, making sure the design that you are working off of is built in a way that allows you to achieve the results. But I think that the piece that often gets forgotten is, how do you manage your people?

Another said,

> I think management is to inspire the people you are working with, to reach, to achieve the mission of the organization. And to walk the walk, to set an example.

A third contributed,

> Management is the structures, the processes, the culture that holds an organization together that enables it to or facilitates its ability to move forward to its mission and vision, and that hopefully also facilitates, or enables the individuals within the organization to bring their full set of gifts to the organization's work and to the larger goals that it's working towards.

Another said,

> Management is strategic vision, management is ensuring collaboration to achieve results. And management is the day to day deliverables. They're ultimately accountable for getting the job done for everybody.

Finally, a manager said,

> It's about investing in people because you're only as good, your organization is only as good, as the people.

People interviewed saw management as an active process that included reaching the mission through concrete actions such as ensuring deliverables, working together, communicating, and holding the vision, along with a commitment of investing in people (staff/team) through inspiring, building trust, being authentic, coaching, mentoring, and role modeling. Managers were seen as responsible for creating a culture within the organization. There was very little about command, control, or managers having the most power and responsibility for decision-making to meet the mission.

Everyone interviewed called for greater linkages within and between divisions and practices within nonprofits. Payroll may seem separate from program, and often the skills of someone in payroll are different than the skills of someone in program; however, both are working for the same ends, and there may be unifying values that will not be discovered without dialogue between departments, one of the more obvious gaps or spaces in between. However, there can also be gaps within operations or program as well; in community development programs, staff working on child rights may not be aware of work being done on gender within the same organization. There are times when these can conflict, and the community can be worse for the mixed messages they are receiving. If finance is operating on systems that are unlinked from payroll and development, redundancies are inevitable, and work is not as efficient.

In the literature, new ideas about managing are replacing old ones, potentially creating multiple cultures or ways of working in one organization if everyone is reading a different book or article and there is no discussion about managing. Newer ideas include support and coaching instead of command. Participation instead of control. Responsibility instead of micromanaging. Communication and coordination instead of fiefdoms and with-holding information. An awareness of the importance of creating an internal culture. Modeling instead of telling. Focusing on how we get to the mission, including by empowering staff, instead of meeting quotas. A willingness for managers to admit mistakes. The managers interviewed for this book stressed the need to *focus on those being managed* as a key component of success, not as an afterthought or rolled into operations or program. If "an organization is only as good as its people", and if "Part of process is working with someone to get to what is important to them" is true for staff as well as those served by the organization, and we are not actively considering them when managing, we are not reaching the mission as successfully as we could be.

In addition to bridging the worker/manager separation, these newer ideas can break down the traditional divide within nonprofits between operations (accomplishing the "hard" tasks, financial reports, payroll, human resources, development, etc.) and program (oversight of service delivery, advocacy, creation of interventions, methodological consistency, report writing), a divide that has been historically reinforced through groups like GuideStar and Charity Navigator in an effort to provide ratings of nonprofits for donors. The higher the percentage spent on program, the higher the charity's rating. Thankfully, this is changing, and perhaps these new definitions of managing, coupled with values, ethics, and process statements, can contribute ideas to what makes a nonprofit donor-worthy.

4.3 Managing and Organizational Structure/Systems/Policies/Functions/Relationships and People

One of the best books on the structure, function, laws, and so on regarding nonprofit management is the *Jossey-Bass Handbook on Nonprofit Management*. It explains almost everything to do with nonprofits from inception through the organizational lifespan. Because that book exists, this book does not need to cover those points, and, really, this book is about a "next step" in nonprofit managing. So get that book as a reference to make sure you know the rules and are clear about all the important things like boards, laws, and finances that are not in these pages (and no, they have not paid me to recommend them, it's just a great book).

Because this management "stuff" is all very intertwined, and because we looked at the historical definitions of management and managing, I thought it might be helpful to look at organizations and their traditional components—structure, systems, policies, and functions—before moving on to the "missing elements"—people and relationships—which are at the heart of all of managing, and are actually the central component of all of our work. Our structure/systems/policies/functions are relational in nature, and they are created by and made up of people. We are, in fact, managing relationships: human, systems, and otherwise, and we are managing people: individuals and teams, to achieve the change we want to see in the world.

4.3.1 Structure

An organization is a group of people coming together to get something done. When the group is small, a formal structure may not be needed; people might take on informal roles based on what needs to be done, their strengths or likes, and the roles are often identified with a specific person. Once the organization becomes larger and legal departments or complex fiscal systems are involved, there may be requirements for officers, higher-level audits, and so on. This is when many groups start to think about a formalized structure, and a unified definition of structure can set the stage for all of the work that follows. Not unlike values and ethics, we may think we are all operating from the same starting point regarding structure, but we may in actuality have deeply differing orientations to structures/structure/levels. Is structure the same as hierarchy? What is the purpose of an organization's structure—does the structure mirror what the organization has been created to do? How do values and ethics inform structure? As time goes on and if the organization grows, its structure may change—is the new component integrated into the old, or is the old structure completely revised resulting in something new? Even more so than the creation of a mission statement, the creation of structure is often not discussed within an organization, there probably is no collective decision-making on this: you are hired to do a job, not to evaluate your organization's structure.

4.3.1.1 Managing as a Way to Unlink Structure and Hierarchy

The most common connection most people make regarding structure is between structure and hierarchy, although in fact structures can be hierarchical, centralized or decentralized, bureaucratic or democratic, top-down or bottom-up. In his recent book, Jacob Morgan (2014) writes about five types of organizational structures: traditional hierarchy, flatter, flat, flatarchies, and holacratic. Other writers link structure and the formal and informal nature of an organization (Chand, 2015). Additional structures include Pre- and Post-Bureaucratic, Matrix, divisional, functional, network. These structures have been developed for a number of reasons, including

- Provision of a "foundation on which standard operating procedures and routines rest" (Jacobides, 2007).
- Providing definition in reporting and role clarity.
- Improvement in operational efficiency—structures "bring organization to the list of work tasks" (Feigenbaum, 2016).
- If people know who does what, and who participates which facet of decision-making, efficiency improves and the job gets done faster.
- Ensuring accountability and measuring results.
- "Departments can work more like well-oiled machines, focusing time and energy on productive tasks" (Ingram, 2016).
- And my favorite: social satisfaction of members (Public Health Action Support Team, 2011).

And as stated in *Organizational Behavior*, structure "defines the form and function of the organization's activities." Structure also defines how the parts of an organization fit together, as in an organizational chart (Griffin and Moorhead, 2014) or an organigram, a map of the systems, jobs, and hierarchy that has been created to achieve the goal based on the organization's size, geography, purpose, and other factors. It illustrates how information is transmitted, who has authority—who reports to whom, and how people within an organization do or do not work together.

Nonprofit organizations come into being because someone or someones saw something that needed to change, or something that needed support or help, and either they set about making that change by themselves, or they needed help (people and systems) and those added components led to the creation of an organization. People in the organization need an understanding of where they fit in to the overall structure, leadership, and who to see to get paid. An organizational chart is developed to map these things. And often the org chart is drafted in a traditional manner with the board at the top, then the executive director (ED), and everyone else below. Which begs the question, is structure the same as hierarchy?

Structure is related to hierarchy in language; organization and organism come from the same root, and structures are inherent to, and needed in, both; an organism is a collection of units, or systems, in some kind of relation to one another, with processes to ensure that the whole survives to reach its goal, which in many cases is reproduction—the continuation of the organism's line. Organizations are also collections of units or systems, at best, created to meet a specific need, to continue to meet that need in situations where need is ongoing, or to cease to be once the need is met.

In an organism, say a fish, there are cells, then groups of "like-minded" cells that form tissue, which result in organs. Organ systems exist side by side and voila! We have an organism. So in a fish, cells form tissue that forms organs, like gills, heart, brain, liver, stomach, air bladder, and so on. They work because of processes, the electrical and chemical occurrences within the fish's systems. There is something in charge: the brain is "telling" the heart to pump, the mouth to open, the tail to swish. These are specific to keeping the fish alive within its environment, whether in the Atlantic Ocean or in a backyard koi pond.

The organization of a rhinoceros, although similar in many ways to that of a fish, is different because it has to function in a different environment. Gills just wouldn't work, nor would there be need for an air bladder. And although the longhorn cowfish and the unicorn fish do have horns, if either had a big, compressed-hair rhino horn it would cause sinkage, and Darwinism would take its course.

One of the things that the fish and the rhino do have in common is that there is a brain/central nervous system in charge, telling the other systems to do their jobs of osmosis, digestion, circulation. Do their jobs or the organism dies. But that's not the end of the story. The fact is that other parts of the fish, ultimately, have a "voice" in whether the little swimmer stays alive or goes to the great fish tank in the sky. Or if the rhino remains on the plains or has an illness in the rains (sorry). If the heart ceases, the brain dies—and so does the rest, whether it is a black rhino or a sardine. Same for the muscular system. Or the circulatory or digestive systems. Each component is critical to the survival of the whole, but because the brain is the one "telling" the others what to do, there is an inherent hierarchy.

Structures exist within living beings, and they exist between beings. Nature is rife with structure that is based on hierarchies; prides of lions, herds of zebras, pods of whales have levels and roles for survival. The hierarchies can be linear or complex, and there are factors that determine where an animal falls in that hierarchy, including age (older > younger), size (larger > smaller), seniority (established member of the group > new member to the group), familial relations (dams > daughters), breed (Angus > Hereford), and the presence, absence, or size of special features like horns, plumage, combs, and tusks (Haynes and Moore-Crawford, 1996).

In human relations, anthropologists posit that our earliest forms of hierarchy were based on age (older), and that strength (more) and gender (male) followed closely. (Ugh. No wonder we're in the mess we're in. Or why there are so many fewer management books written by women and organizations look and act like they do. We haven't come as far as we think we have, although slowly, *slowly* we are getting better.) Later, religion became a touchstone for hierarchy and caste.

Because of what is in our DNA, our cultural conditioning, evolution, what we have observed and what we value, and because we want to move from confusion to understanding, organizations have most often been hierarchical in structure: It has been what we've known, and we've accepted it. Use of hierarchy for organizational structure is both objective and subjective and includes the need to comply with laws, maintaining the organization's vision, having an overview of how the organization is functioning, a reliance on existing structural models, and the environment in which the organization is seated.

Coming from the "old school," my experience is that structure in general, and especially within organizations, is important. People want to know where they fit in and how the organization is set up so that they can do their jobs in relation to others who know where they fit in and how the organization is set up so they can do their jobs. It's helpful. None of the people interviewed for this book thought organizational structure should not exist (although the idea of breaking up the international mega-organizations to lessen northern-based overheads and increase inclusion of impacted populations by being closer to the ground did come up). But structure and the formal idea of hierarchy do not have to be one in the same. In living things, there is a biological hierarchy. In much of human interaction, as we've discussed previously, our hierarchies and their accompanying ideas, values, and behaviors have been defined and imposed by other humans, in part because, as Darwin noted, hierarchies get things done.

In a study looking at the efficacies of flat versus steep hierarchies, it appears that steep hierarchies help groups succeed when the work they are doing is routine and does not require inputs from group members. If a group has come together to undertake complex or less-defined tasks, a steep hierarchy is not helpful to good results. Good results were also hindered when a group leader was corrupt in using their power. Authors list the following factors that can impact the effectiveness of hierarchy:

■ The kinds of tasks on which the group is working
■ Whether the right individuals have been selected as leaders
■ How the possession of power modifies leaders' psychology

- Whether the hierarchy facilitates or hampers intra-group coordination
- Whether the hierarchy affects group members' motivation in positive or deleterious ways (Anderson and Brown, 2010)

Based on research literature and experience, much of hierarchy has been defined by ideas of power, authority, leadership, and control.

4.3.1.1.1 Hierarchy, Power, Authority, Leadership, and Control

Once you are supervising people, power relationships change, and everyone knows this. My father worked for Anheuser-Busch for 40 years, and at one point, they wanted to make him a foreman. He declined because he didn't want to be anyone's boss, he wanted to continue to be one of the crew even though it would have meant more money if he took the promotion. He knew the power dynamics and decided he did not want to be on the management side. And, say what you want about unions, he would have had to leave the union which had made it possible for him to have vacations, health insurance, and a feeling of camaraderie with his coworkers—he belonged to something bigger than himself that benefited many, and he was very clear about his decision.

One could say that both leaders and authorities—like managers—have some measure of power, either assigned by social norms or freely bestowed by people who are moved to follow a person or people to some end (or beginning). Power can be wielded like a club, or it can rest gently, increasing marginally when needed, to move closer to the vision. There is so much wrapped up in this, ideas that managers have about how things should be done, ideas that staff have about how things should be done, ways in which donors think things should be done, and ideas of how those served think things should be done. Then there is the law—how a given government sets laws and policies around the functioning of a nonprofit. Everyone has an idea of how things should be done. So whose idea is right? And keeping within the power discussion, who has the power to decide?

Even in the flattest structures/hierarchies, there is most often someone with a bit more authority—a flat hierarchy can be a cover for some very manipulative manifestations in an organization. My husband once worked in a company that stated they had a flat hierarchy and what that really meant was that the CEO felt she could "contribute" (meddle) in all aspects of the corporation, changing things on a whim, not sticking to policy. This is an inauthentic way to maintain control, by keeping everyone off-balance and guessing as to what was coming next. If you want a flatter hierarchy, maybe leadership rotates, maybe titles are not used, but *someone* has to start things moving. Or stop them if they are moving away from the process and mission.

In the private sector, there are estimates that a good leader, who can hold the vision of the company and structure systems and people so that they work most effectively, can add an additional 10 percent to the bottom line. Is leadership the same thing as authority? Writers on this subject would say no; leadership is holding a vision greater than yourself and being able to motivate people to accomplish that vision. Authority is most often based on a role that has significance in a specific context, such as an Imam or a policy officer. A person can be a leader while holding a position of authority, or a person can be authoritarian—my way or the highway—in a leadership position.

Authority, power, leadership, and control are based on relationship. One of the base premises of this book is actually a version of what Craig Dowden (2013) calls version 2.0 of the Golden Rule: "treat others as *they* want to be treated," instead of treat others as you want to be treated. And although that may sound like the goal is to be nice to everyone, to help everyone, I would say that what it really means is that different people need different things to be successful. If you do unto others as *they* want, you are not limiting ways of interacting to what is acceptable to *you*. You are interacting with another entity (I-Thou and not I-It) so that something new might happen. As a manager, sometimes this includes being supportive, encouraging, listening, and sometimes that means helping someone to move to a different organization where they will be of better service to those for whom the organization is working. And I really mean *helping* the person move on, not pushing them out, but working with them to help them move on. There are times when a person does something that is significantly outside the boundaries of ethics and/or the law; in these instances, termination needs to be implemented immediately. However, in over 20 years of managing or running not-for-profit organizations, I have seen this happen three times: once when there were founded allegations of sexual abuse, once when someone had given another staff person unprescribed prescription drugs from a medical center, and once when someone was embezzling funds. It does happen, but incidences are few and far between.

If the policies, methods, and behaviors within our organizations comingle structure with hierarchy, we are conflating structure and hierarchy within our institutions and pushing that out into the world.

But, you might say, isn't hierarchy implicit in structure? And I'd respond, it all depends on your mission and the world you want to see.

If the organizational culture dictates that structure is the same as hierarchy, that all mandates and decisions come from the top and there's not a lot of feedback, then structure and hierarchy are the same. If there are feedback mechanisms, participatory decision-making, open doors, and role clarity, structure lets you know where you fit in and allows you to contribute across the organization. It also demands that you are aware of what is happening in other parts of the organization so that you can make informed contributions. In this instance, structure and hierarchy become less linked.

4.3.1.1.2 Unlinking Structure and Hierarchy

Let's start from the idea that everyone has a form of efficacy, that everyone has some thought or fraction of a thought that could change the world, that everyone has a little piece of the "truth," as Mills wrote (1869). Including you. And let's say that our experience showed us that unless we gather those pieces of truth, important pieces of information are going to be missing. What if we started from the perspective that everyone has something to offer to the big picture, everyone has an idea to spread, not unlike TED's mission statement? What if we were not afraid that we would lose what we have by reaching out to others, but that we would be enriched by it? As managers, we could be enriched by the knowledge contributed by our team and use that for the good of the mission. Our willingness to listen, a transparent way of working and treating everyone as they would be treated, would be the basis for our authority. Inspiring one's team to do the best work they can by doing the best work you can would eliminate the need for control. The idea is that this could lead to less restructuring in both for- and nonprofit organizations because structure and hierarchy would be uncoupled, and we would be able to see and address any actual structural problems in an organization.

Managers can demonstrate the idea of structure uncoupled from hierarchy. They live in two worlds. They are part of the neural system, transmitting information to keep the system functioning, and are part of a specific system within the structure (circulatory, digestive, etc.), monitoring that system so that the organization is functioning properly. They are collectors, relayers, and receivers of information within the structure so there can be an ordered way of getting the job done and acknowledging that every part of the organism is contributing to the functioning of the whole. Managers can demonstrate ways in which staff can work that empower them instead of diminishing them. And they can even do it within more traditional systems, policies, and functions.

4.3.2 Systems, Policies, and Functions

… this is where the structure becomes just crazy.
Because the staffing of [the organization] is 60 percent short-term like myself who have contracts with
no benefits and we are more than half of the total
staff. So when it comes to things like this like the
restructure, we're not actually involved, we are not
asked what we think. We're only told after and even
then they don't have much to say. There is an abso-
lute lack of trust and accountability within [the orga-
nization] which means that they counter that with
compliance. So there's so many systems of compliance, there's so many tasks and processes related to
reporting and to managing up to your manager, to
their manager, to their manager, managing people's
egos and politics and agendas, so this 60 percent
plus of people that are working in the organization
on short-term contract are basically invisible … they
did away with long-term consultants. So now there's
nothing so it's made the hierarchy even worse. So
they're looking only at the systems level, they're not
looking at the interaction level, of what it means to
have certain types of contractual arrangements, of
what it means certain types of reporting arrangements. (Interviewee)

I've pulled this quote from one of the interviews to illustrate
the bridge between structure and systems/policies/functions. In
this case, the bridge seems to be between Bosch's *Garden of
Earthly Delights* (specifically the right-hand panel as you view
the painting) and Dante's Seventh to Ninth Circles of Hell. This
is a large international organization with strict hierarchy with
no room for advancement (and no health insurance), internal
competition for scarce resources, egos that need to be managed, lack of accountability resulting in additional compliance

systems, lack of trust, ego managing, uncertainty, no opportunity to input into structural or systems decision-making, egos. In essence, an organization where restructuring and the ongoing creation of systems to support that restructuring has become an end in itself, and is being done to ignore or avoid looking at internal problems and how its structure, systems, policies, and functions create an internal world that, in the case of this organization, can spill out to the larger world where it works and has led to further division and inequity.

Let's drill down into systems, policies, and functions, because these are parts of managing.

When we think about organizational systems we most often think about internal groups like Finance, Payroll, Human Resources, Fundraising, IT, Operations, Legal.

Policies are the codified ways that delineate how organizations and systems operate. They can be dictated by law, for example U.S. organizations are not supposed to hire people who are not documented in the U.S.. On the other hand, the Americans with Disabilities Act (ADA) ensured that people with disabilities could not face discrimination when it came to hiring, and sexual harassment is legally banned because it is a form of sex discrimination. Others policies are internal to an organization, like how travel is paid—with a credit card, through a cash advance, or by the staff person for later reimbursement—or whether people can work from home or how much vacation they are allowed.

Function is defined here as the ways policies within systems are interpreted and implemented; policies should be implemented consistently across the organization.

Each organizational system is responsible for something specific, and has a way of getting there that is encoded in its policies and operationalized through its functions. The finance department has (or should have) policies around how checks are handled, how reimbursement forms are filled out, how payroll is managed, how grants are recorded. And although some of the policies apply almost exclusively to the specific department—like actually assigning salary amounts and cutting paychecks (my age is showing—make that direct depositing pay), systems, policies, and functions interlink between and are dependent on other systems/departments. What is the point of a payroll system if there are no staff to pay? Or of a program delivery system if there are no resources? Systems, policies, and functions, by their very nature, are relational. Finance needs to keep track of the money, Payroll needs Finance's information to cut paychecks, and staff in Finance is paid by Payroll.

How effectively systems are operating through their policies and functions, or are viewed to be operating, impacts overall organizational decision-making. One interviewee talked about how the perceived need for a better financial system and oversight impacted CEO hiring:

> … I remember when I first joined the organization, that was the first CEO that had come from the business world, and he had been asked to come rather than from the not-for-profit, because they felt that the financial part was becoming a little too shaky, and they needed someone from the business world to try to control all of these, whatever was happening there … he came in to control the finances. It [the organization] was becoming too much of the heart, that they needed a strict business thing. So this guy had a very authoritarian style, I don't know if everyone wanted him out, [but] he was asked to leave. He managed the finances, he laid out a very nice system, and there was still a lot of freedom in that, but the structure in the organization, the way things were going, it was becoming very top-heavy, the headquarters changed from one country to another country and became very top-heavy and there was no way you could keep the salaries the same, and a whole lot of things started changing, programs

> started changing, and the way the organization
> is right now, I think that unless the organization
> changes in structure, going to be very difficult for it
> to continue.

This is a great example of how an emphasis on one system and its functions, without the inclusion of other departments, the organizational culture, and how systems interact within the organization, can significantly change an organization's orientation. Systems, policies, and functions by their nature are relational. If a CEO focuses on one (finance) to the exclusion or diminishment of another (program), the overall organization will be misaligned, out of whack. It would be like the entire medical profession concentrating on the digestive system and its functions, and while this would be amazing for people with stomach ulcers, people with arthritis or ear infections may not be as happy or supportive.

Systems, including policies and functions, need a "systems approach," which means that systems are not seen in isolation, as static or as siloed entities. The policies and functions within systems need to be considered in relation to both their own system and also between one another, how they relate, how they reinforce or detract from one another. It's very similar to the ideas within family systems theory that we discussed earlier. The idea of a systems approach reorients systems, policies, and functions from solely the nuts and bolts of what one system needs to do to, to the idea of "process," considering *how* organizational systems, processes, and functions work by themselves as well as how they relate to others. If one part of a system is not functioning well, we need to look at whether there is a specific issue within that system (policy/function/individual/group), whether the problem is between systems (human resources and legal or program and fundraising), or whether we need to look at the whole organization and consider how the systems, policies, and methods came to be, and why they exist as they do.

As an example, let's say that people in Organization C are having trouble getting reimbursed for expenditures. From both inside and outside the finance system, it seem that the problem is the individual responsible for reimbursements; however, it would be helpful to take a look at the system/systems within which the person is working to help delineate whether the problem is actually with the person or with the system. Are reimbursement forms complicated? Is petty cash available? Does the person have multiple responsibilities in addition to reimbursements? Are there enough resources? Who has made the decisions that impact the department? Are job descriptions clear? Is the person unable to carry out the tasks of the position? If so, why?

Getting to the cause of the problem that leads to slow reimbursement is critical if the problem is to be solved, otherwise we may be blaming an individual when there are systemic problems, or systemic problems when the job is not a good fit for the individual. Perhaps leadership feels that 95 percent of resources have to be directed toward program so that the organization's Charity Navigator rating is four-star.* Or the accounting software purchased is not adequate for the tasks at hand (or maybe it's way too much program for the organization, and people are really confused and are afraid to say they can't use it because of the investment that has been made). The point is that unless we know what the problem is, we can't create a workable solution, and if we are not looking at the places where systems and functions intersect and interact, we may be proposing a solution that will not solve the problem. As a manager, you are going to want to look for the causes of problems in order to try to solve them.

Managers can be interpreters of systems and can work to ensure equity in systems, policy, and functions. They can be the grease between systems so that things move along more

---

* Guide Star is, fortunately, revamping its charity rating system to include more than just overhead to program ratios.

smoothly. They can be the conduit through which information flows, knowing and understanding policies and explaining existing systems and functions to their teams. They can work to ensure that policies and functions within their system are created within the law, are modified in collaboration with their team, and are clear, known, and applied fairly to all.

If your organization has dealt with these issues—and others—then staff are probably clear about what is possible and what is not at any given point in time. And if you as staff don't like the possible, then you might want to work for someone else, or you might want to read Saul Alinsky and advocate for internal systems and/or policy change.

4.4 Managing, Relationships, and People

The missing elements of traditional management literature are relationships and people. It's so interesting that older definitions of managing/management don't specifically include people and relationships, because those are its essence, what managing is all about. This is changing as reflected in the recent literature on managing, which includes people and relationships as part of a manager's priorities. It is true that your organization is only as good as the people who work within it and, I would add, only as good as the relationships between people, systems, structures, and so on. Richard Branson, founder of the Virgin empire, is committed to this idea, as were Teddy Roosevelt and Peter Drucker. If we want good relationships outside our workplaces, we have to live them inside our workplaces.

I'm sure that you can see the relevance of both people and relationships in each of the aforementioned areas: we will act in a different way toward one another if we uncouple structure and hierarchy; equity of policy application creates a level playing field on which we can meet as equals; understanding roles—ours and others—lets us know who to talk to for what purpose; input into the creation of structures, systems, and policies will have an impact both on functions and on how we treat others (hopefully positive). So let's move to the act of managing, where we'll first take a look at relationships and people.

4.5 The Act of Managing

So far we've talked about managing primarily from a traditional definition that includes structures, systems, policies, and methods. We've looked at strengths and weaknesses of each and have emphasized the need for a focus on people and interrelationships—the spaces in between.

The components described will impact a nonprofit's mission by how they relate (or do not relate) to one another. We need systems and policies and methods if a nonprofit is to meet its mission and retain its nonprofit status (complying with existing laws and regulations), and we are going to need some sort of structure. And this is where the act of managing comes in. Managing is in fact quite important, because someone has to have their eye on both the big picture, and on making sure the work gets done; not for self-aggrandizement, but so that the systems (created and run by people) within systems within systems are relating, and the "whole" is moving toward the mission in a way that reflects the world we want to see. It involves leadership.

If you are a manager, you are also a leader, and your actions as a manager will speak louder than any words you will say. People interviewed emphasized the idea that management includes leadership and vice versa, that they are indivisible.

One interviewee said,

> Okay well here's the thing. I think they absolutely are connected, leadership and management, and I

think that the way that many NGOs operate, and not only NGOs, I think this is also true for the non-NGO side, I think that the way many organizations operate are disconnected … you said management, not effective management.

If you are managing the relationships of people, systems, policies, structures, and functions, you have to coordinate, inspire, walk the walk, have integrity, move the organization forward, invest in staff, hold the vision and mission, collaborate, create processes, ensure deliverables and accountability, create clear lines of reporting, make decisions. You have to be consistent, keep negative ideas or problems with other staff to yourself, stay strong, and not use your staff as a personal or professional support system. And do budgeting and write reports—I forgot those. Managing is more than an act, it's a three-ring circus; hopefully a well-timed, organized circus.

One of the first questions we need to ask regarding the act of managing is why, what, and who are we managing, for what purpose, and how do we relate to and/or perform in a management role?

4.5.1 Why Are We Managing?

Hopefully, we are managing because there is a need for coordination and support. Given the program work, methods, policies, systems, structures, relationships, values, behaviors, and size of the organization, there will need to be a person or persons to coordinate, to keep an eye out to make sure all of these components are leading to the achievement of the mission.

Managers are needed to provide information and support their team(s) so that work can get done, as well as to keep track of what's being done and the results; it is, at its best, an uncoupling of hierarchy and structure for the benefit of the work. In a traditional organizational pyramid, the manager is at the top and the staff/team are below. That might be ok for the organizational chart, but if you are managing as mission, a manager might be included at the bottom, or in the middle, or around the outside of their team. Staff have questions and need to ask someone. They run up against a closed door and need someone to help open it (inside or outside the organization). Their manager can advocate with "higher-ups" for change when something is not working, or when someone has a great idea that can be implemented. Managers are needed to mediate workplace conflicts when staff cannot do it themselves, or when systems are in conflict with one another. They are sometimes needed to act as a buffer between those higher-up in the organization and staff working with those served. And they can be a sounding board for venting and problem-solving.

If the organization is small enough, managers, even structure, may not be needed. Why waste scarce resources on a position that does not contribute to the mission? But when things get unwieldy, or when someone has too much in their job description, or if bills are not being paid on time, it's time to ask if something needs to change. Staff should have a voice in the decision-making regarding structure because they see the gaps from a different perspective than more senior staff and have valuable inputs. The CEO or director can also refer to the board and/or a consultant for advice, if appropriate.

If there is a need for managers, we need clarity on what and who we are managing.

4.5.2 What/Who Are We Managing?

We are managing a whole lot of things: tasks, people, deadlines, timelines, finances, processes, hiring, firing, procedures, systems, systems within systems, structures, relationships, values, and behaviors, all the things that we've discussed. And ourselves. We are managing ourselves in our work and our relation to the work, in relation to systems, structures, policies, and functions. We are managing relationships. As in Buber. I-Thou.

In addition to all of the specifics just listed, managing is very much about looking at the spaces between structures, people, systems, and so on. What comes out of the places where they touch on one another? What is the quality of inter-actions and outputs from those interactions? Are there places where there are conflicts? Where things run smoothly and easily? Or where things are being slowed down (bottlenecks)? If the organization is experiencing problems, we might want to start an investigation into the spaces in between, where relationships happen. What or who touches what or who, and what are the results, because that is a big part of what needs to be managed inside and outside a nonprofit, and how the management of those relationships best reflect the mission/ goal we are trying to achieve.

Remember the "Levels" list from the chapter on Process? Here is a two-step exercise for you. First, let's take a step away from hierarchy and structure and think of these as relationships instead of levels. Then, using that list (reproduced next), add the people and things (processes, systems, etc.) not listed that you might imagine having to manage or are currently managing. Please do not feel constrained by the number of blank spaces, write in as many or as few as you can think of—add lines, get a notepad. You can change this list in any way you'd like:

- Person to themselves (including you)
- Staff to you as manager
- You to staff as manager
- Staff to staff
- Staff to those served
- Those served to staff
- Staff to the work
- You to finance
- You to fundraising

- Finance to you
- Fundraising to you
- Staff to finance
- Finance to staff
- Staff to mission and vision
- You to external systems
- External systems to you
- External systems to external systems that impact staff/work/organization
- _____
- _____
- _____
- _____
- _____

Now that you have *your* list, step two is to determine if there is interaction, if there needs to be interaction, what the current interaction involves, and then translate that interaction into the idea of relationship. Write your mission at the top of the page, choose one interaction, then ask yourself the questions:

- How do these interactions take place now?
- How might these interactions be viewed as "I-Thou" relationships?
- How would viewing them as relationships, as a reflection of the mission, change the way interactions take place?

Here is an example of how to do this:

Mission of my organization: To reduce infant mortality in urban areas using an epidemiological approach.

As a manager, I interact with members of my team.

1. Right now, we meet as a team, in the conference room, every two weeks and everyone goes around and gives a brief update of what they have been doing. I talk with each of them once a week in my office with the door closed. During

our meetings, I ask that they have an agenda and a checklist of the work they have done. I suggest articles and other literature for them to read about the work, new methodologies, program ideas. There is a calendar of events that everyone knows about but some things get lost like reports that are due. We have monthly birthday parties to celebrate. Any one of them can knock on my office door if they have a question.

2. If I were going to see my interaction with staff as I-Thou, I would probably ask more questions about whether the format of our team meetings and weekly meetings is helpful, and make considered changes based on what I hear. I might also ask if a centralized file, where everyone can share articles and so on, would be helpful. I might also ask if the calendar is effective and, if not, what would be helpful. Finally, I'd ask if the monthly party is what people want, or if there is something else that would be more enjoyable.

3. As a reflection of mission, these changes would allow for my staff to have input into decisions, and this could help staff feel ownership of the work and build critical thinking skills. This could translate into thinking regarding the inclusion of critical thinking skills within programmatic intervention. Maybe some people really like the checklist idea, and maybe some would like to structure our meetings in other ways—this would meet individual needs without much effort and reflect the idea that one size does not fit all, again to spur thinking about contextualizable intervention methods.

And although you don't have to manage relationships between each of the dyads on your list all the time—or your dyad may be a triad or a quadral or a pentad (I had to look those last two up) or you may be managing three or four of the dyads at a given time—you will definitely have to manage *yourself* all the time, which can be the most difficult of all because the way you manage yourself will be the example you set and the message you send to staff, systems, structures, and will provide an illustration of the boundaries within which those around you will allow themselves to do the work.

The spaces in between people, systems, structures, departments, roles, and so on are where the *how*, the *process*, that needs to be managed takes place; the exchanges, the rubs, the ideas. If we want a world that is more equitable and sustainable, we need to look at the relationships within our organizations, at the spaces in between the work where values-based behaviors meet, link, clash, explode, mesh, grind, produce, limit, expand, and impact individuals, programs, systems, structures, policies, and functions.

4.5.3 You—Managing

As a manager, your job is to make sure work gets done so that the mission can be met. You have to look at the big picture, hold the mission and vision, ensure adherence to policies, negotiate between systems, sometimes between people, give feedback (hopefully positive and constructive [how to do better]), hire, fire, all the things we've talked about. And I guarantee you that things are going to push your buttons; you are going to react, you are going to get angry, frustrated, startled ... as one of the interviewees said, "*whatever demons you have, they will come ... and be with you all the time.*"

If you are reading this book (and because your eyes are falling on these words I'm imaging you are), you may be at the beginning of your nonprofit managing career. You may be a manager wanting some ideas on how to manage in a different way. You want to meet the mission. You see the link between how people are treated and subsequently, how they treat others. You are open to learn. You have made mistakes. You want people to succeed. You are primed to do a good job. Thank you. The world is already a better place with you in it. You are my people.

Managing is a huge amount of work, both internally and externally. Which leads to the question: Has anyone ever asked you if you want to manage? Have you asked yourself? Do you want to be dealing with all the relationships and problems? Because this is a choice—you don't have to have the bulk of your job as management. It is truly, totally, wonderfully helpful, needed, appropriate, to want to do program work and not to want to manage others. So if all of this added stuff does not appeal to you, I fully support you. We need to pay the direct service workers more so that we can retain expertise and professionalism in those roles. Like paying teachers as the professionals they are—it's a no-brainer.

Did anyone ask you if you know how to manage? To lead? What a new position of authority means to you and to those you work with? Has anyone explained the structures and systems with which you and your staff will need to interact? The expectation may be that you will know how to do all of them because you are good at your direct service or program work job. Have you had any training in any of these areas? Or are you expected to know all of this without experience or training, like Athena springing fully formed from the head of Zeus? Maybe without the owl.

When asked whether their workplace provided opportunities to discuss management strategies, one interviewee stated,

> the company as a whole implemented 360 feedback, how people above below and alongside you felt that you were performing different functions, and there were also a couple of tests like the Myers-Briggs test, there was another one that didn't focus so much on personality type but focused on communication styles that they gave us, so there were a number of things like that that we would do that would help us reflect either on our work or how our style of work

was perceived by others, or how our makeup was likely to influence our work, what was helpful about that or what needed to be worked on.

People accept managing roles for many reasons—they want to move ahead, they want to make more money, they feel they have no choice but to supervise (and maybe they don't). It's unfair for us in the nonprofit world to expect that a person will know how to do these things if we don't provide training for them. And it's not good for the mission. If effective leadership increases the bottom line by 10 percent, and if we can make a gross generalization that the same might apply to the nonprofit sector, then we are shortchanging the people/cause served by the organization. We are not doing our best. We need to invest in our staff people as we would invest in those we serve.

Managing can happen to you because of an immediate need; grant funding comes in and new people have to be hired. Staff who are doing the actual work (you), be it advocacy, community development, or social case work, are suddenly tasked with managing people. It happens all the time. We think that managing staff is no big deal, you did the job, you know how to do it, you know the population you serve, what's the problem? The problem is that you may *not* know. And the idea that you should know sets up an expectation that can be transmitted down the line—if you are expected to know and you don't, you might expect your staff to know and they might not. Which can move further down the line to those served, and new staff may expect people to do things that they don't know how to do.

The jump from doing the work to managing others doing the work is significant. People have different values and behaviors and react differently to perceived authority. Maybe you were "one of the workers," and now you are their boss. Your now-former peers may be working for very different reasons than those that brought you to the job. Their concept of time and time management may diverge from your ideas. They probably have strengths in areas that are not your strong suits, and weaknesses in areas you take for granted. You may like them very much, or not like them at all. Maybe they want your job. Maybe they are now doing your job better than you did it.

And you have to interact with systems that in the past may not have been necessary for the achievement of your work. Human Resources. Finance. Fundraising/Development. Your satisfaction and frustrations no longer come from direct service work but from other sources. And where before you may have had to manage relationships with and between those served, you now have to manage relationships with and between staff and systems. You have become part of the institutional structure and are responsible for working with and motivating others to ensure that deliverables are met. You have become the hub of a wheel, moving in from being a spoke. It's a lot, right?

Don't panic. Learning all this takes time—time that you probably don't have a lot of given this list of areas for which you are now responsible. Hopefully, your organization has materials and policies around managing; if not, the internet is chock-full of articles. You will learn it. And hopefully, you will leave the organization and the world a little better than you found it. If you want to accomplish this, humility is essential, or you will recreate a management system that translates into a way of working with those the organization serves, that reflects a top-down, neo-colonial way of operating that is an incredibly large part of why the world is in its current mess. I know humility was not a popular idea with the Khmer Rouge or with Josef Stalin or _____ (fill in the blank with your favorite tyrant), but you know what happens when there is a lack of humility and a lust for power.

Over time, you will develop a management style. It's sort of like a musician or artist developing a musical or painting niche/style; however, artists are free to move in directions that don't necessarily impact anyone other than themselves through sales and/or reputation. If one musician in a band wants to move in a direction that does not work for the other band members, the band breaks up. If this happens in the nonprofit management world, you may find yourself out of a job or deeply unhappy. Unlike the notoriety that can go with great art, or the money that can accompany for-profit management, great management in nonprofits is behind the scenes and, because we don't have the "*Managing Grammys*" or a *Pulitzer* for Team Leads, motivated, productive, supported staff with better outcomes has to be its own reward.

The caveat here is that management styles are largely a reflection of one's experience and personality, unless there is an organizational culture demanding a specific way of interacting. Research has shown that there is a correlation between a manager's personality, their leadership style, and their capacity to lead for change (Alkahtani et al., 2011). Meyers–Briggs, The Caliper Profile, and Gallup Strengths Finder are some of the personality tests being used by human resource departments to determine goodness of fit for specific roles (Chatterjee, 2015). According to the Society for Human Resource Management, over 60 percent of human resource departments in the for-profit sector are using personality tests prior to hiring (Meinert, 2015).

Sometimes, people thoroughly embody a specific style and use it to the exclusion of others, which may work for some team members, but this has the potential to alienate others who don't respond to that style. Why is this important? A recent Gallup poll indicated that in a study of 7,200 people, 50 percent quit because of their manager (Snyder, 2015). Additional surveys indicate that managers and leadership are the main reasons why people quit. Article titles include "People Leave Managers, Not Companies" (Lipman, 2015a), "Employees Quit Leaders, Not Companies" (Hassell, 2013).

If you look at articles like these on the web, the pictures of Kevin Spacey and Jason Bateman from *Horrible Bosses* are often used to illustrate the idea. In that movie, Kevin Spacey is demeaning, self-serving, narcissistic, humiliating, inflexible, sadistic. His personality is bordering on sociopathic. *Don't be like him*.

As an example of the need for flexibility in managing styles, an interviewee stated,

> to be an effective manager, you must always be willing yourself to do the task that you are delegating. One of the greatest ways for a manager to develop a rapport and trust with their staff is for the staff to be confident that when their manager is asking something of them, that person knows what the ask means. They know what it entails, truly, to accomplish that project, including the scope of work and potential burdens, and how it could impact the employee's current work load. It's also vital that staff be able to trust that there's a reason behind a manager's ask. Staff members need to know that there's value behind the work being asked of them and that managers are not just making arbitrary decisions or delegating projects on a whim. For a manager to be in tune with the workload of their staff, and to be in tune with the full scope and magnitude of what they are actually asking is really important because this knowledge helps to limit employee burnout. Burnout is a mission killer. You lose your staff, you lose your motivation, you lose that drive and that passion.

If you think your personality does not impact on your work as a manager, it's time for us to talk. I mean it. *Call me.* As a long-time manager and consultant said,

[this is important because you need to] be in a place
of connection with yourself, and be in a place where
you are actually leading from wisdom and active
choice instead of emotional reactivity.

There will be people who pooh-pooh the idea that their
personality impacts managing, and that they do not need to
look at themselves within the context of their work. In very
rare cases, it may happen that one's personality lends itself
perfectly to managing everyone on their team and relationships within a specific organization. VERY rare cases. For
most of us, we have to be willing to adapt or change based
on what we see in front of us. If we think we don't have to
change and adapt as a manager, and we expect change from
the people we serve—we expect drug use to stop, domestic
violence to cease, the Japanese to stop killing whales, gun
laws to change (it's been too many pages since I mentioned
gun control)—and have not ourselves been willing to change,
we lack credibility and an understanding of what it means for
others. Hey, we are the helpers! We've got it together enough
to work to help others. We've gone to school, are special and
important, and have a higher calling. That's why we are where
we are—like Mary Poppins, "practically perfect in every way."
The problem is that 50 percent of staff quit because of their
managers. Good people quit. People who have expertise and
commitment. People with integrity. Statistics prove the point.

Like those who are served by our organizations, we have
to be willing to change, to manage so the mission is met. To
look at what happens in between us and the people and systems we are managing and acknowledge the things we bring,
both helpful and not so helpful, and the things "thou" brings,
helpful and not so helpful, and be willing to change how we
interact to change what happens in that space in between. As
manager, it is our job to "hold that space," work to make it
safe, open, equal, so that something in the best interest of the
mission can happen. It does not mean that as manager one

backs down or denies knowledge and/or experience. It does mean that one might be willing to suspend judgment and really listen to a person, even when what we are hearing does not mesh with what we know/experience. An interviewee said,

> That's the problem, people have to connect in some way. But people also have to be willing to change. And they have to be willing to at least be open to hearing other points of view if management is going to be successful, if it's going to mirror the world I want to see. And so I think that by and large people are scared to death to change, they're scared to death to hear other people's opinions, they're scared to really take it in, really absorb it. They are threatened in some way.

If someone has a different idea, comes from a different culture, or has a different set of values than you, listening and questioning might lead to a new idea, a different way to do something. If you are open to this as a manager, you will be fostering critical thinking in your staff, and this, as far as I'm concerned, is part of the world we want to see. It shows an openness, and lets people know *you* are willing and able to change.

CHANGE AND DONUTS

And now an example of difficult personal change. I love Krispy Kreme vanilla-filled glazed donuts. When I was commuting into NYC, every weekday I walked past the Krispy Kreme stand in Penn Station and I would often indulge. It was so hard not to respond to that Krispy Kreme vanilla-filled glazed donut when it was calling my name. LORI ... LORI ... LOOK, I'M RIGHT OVER HERE ... I'M SO GOLDEN AND SWEET AND FLUFFY LIKE A PERFECT PILLOW OF GLAZED SUGAR AND DOUGH AND CREAMY

DELICIOUSNESS ... LORI .... It was often impossible to say no. And then my weight started to creep up. Creep creep creep. Up up up. At some point, I had to change my behavior, to hear that donut, look it squarely in the cream and say, "Vanilla Crème donut, I love you and I want you as much as you want me ... right now ... but we will have to wait ... we have to delay gratification and I will visit next week and perhaps then our love can be consummated—I mean consumed. I mean I will EAT YOU! Well, not *you* because you will be old and stale by that time. One of your companion donuts." I hated it. I started saying no to the donut (but we all know donuts can't talk so I said no to myself). And I lost the weight I had gained and I'm sure my pancreas is much happier.

Change can be hard. Saying no to that lovely donut is hard. Listening to the better angels of my nature is hard. It is an internal battle, me telling myself not to do something and me reacting because I want to do it. It sets up a dissonance that moves to an internal conflict that, even if I win—wait, it's internal, I have to win—*and* lose, leaves me either a little exhausted and frustrated and maybe a bit edgier than I would ordinarily be, or victorious both in the moment when I say no, and again when I step on the scale. Or all of the above.

If the dissonance comes from outside, if someone disagrees or gives a better solution to a problem, especially if the person is "beneath" you in the organizational structure, and particularly if there are other staff around, it might hurt and hurt/humiliation/frustration can easily lead to anger. Or it may not be what a person says, it may be in the way that they say it that triggers your anger. It can feel demeaning, like you've fallen off your pedestal, like you are wrong, you don't know, as if someone else might know something different, something better. It feels like there is a lot at stake. We might be afraid of losing what we have worked so hard for—our position, our expertise, our credibility—if we admit that we don't know, or that someone might have a better idea, or that we are not right. But in managing, if you are not willing to be open to changing, to growing even when it hurts, you are maintaining the status quo. There is too much at stake to maintain stasis.

This is one of the key messages of *Managing As Mission*: you have to be open to change. And then you have to take the steps to make the change happen. It's one of the reasons that there are so many books on management out there full of tools and guides and charts, because it's easier to try a new strategic planning method than it is to have to change internally. One of the interviewees said it best:

> I think the one thing I would say is that I think the internal piece is so important, internal to the person, because when I think about when I was in previous leadership positions, and I had access to good training programs, and all of that, so much of the training focus is on skills, like management skills. How you can structure your meeting differently in this way, or here's a template for decision-making or that kind of stuff, these tools, best practices and that kind of thing. And some of those things were helpful, and there are just so many of them and ultimately who in a leadership position has so much time to be spending reading books and all of that?
>
> So I think that the thing that I felt that was really missing for me was the place to be internally courageous ... there's not a lot of support for that kind of being real with yourself in those kinds of positions. It's incredibly lonely, secondly it feels like there's so much risk in honesty and being too reflective sometimes; it's more than just your personal opinion. There's a lot riding on stuff. And it's so easy, all those tools gave me permission to shut the interior stuff down, it gave me permission to say, "No,

I should read this book about how to structure my
meetings differently or what's the best strategic planning process," or whatever, so it kept reinforcing to
me that the answer was outside somewhere, and yes
that stuff is important and useful, but it can never
replace the interior stuff, interior work of being able
to be with yourself, having that place of total honesty
with yourself, not running from yourself, not running from all those triggers that are following you
around all over. And being able to articulate "what
is my truth?" in any given situation. So that may not
be ultimately what the decision is, but you have to
at least know what that is. So that's the only thing I
would say; there's so much focus in leadership circles
around external stuff. And not enough space and
respect for the interior work that leaders really have
to do to really bring their full gifts to the leadership
opportunity.

It is critical to be introspective—not navel-gazing, but self-
assessing; bad management can be due to a lack of internal
honesty/introspection, caused by someone not knowing how
to manage because they never learned, or can be an outcome of dysfunctional systems. If a system is not designed to
be open and adaptable to change (buzzword: nimble), it will
recreate what exists, both inside in how it treats its staff, and
outside in what it produces or the actions it takes, and how it
treats those with whom it is working/serving.

One of the interviewees illustrated this point in the following conversation:

Interviewee: [there is a] … total lack of accountability. But it's
also not surprising that there is no focus on actually
managing people, being a supervisor or coach or
mentor, because you're all competing for the same

time and attention and the vast majority of that attention is looking upwards and not down to you.

Lori: And then how does that impact the mission?

Interviewee: Everybody is just a cog in this giant wheel right?
And this is part of the lack of trust, which directly
impacts the mission and how people are doing their
jobs. People, again, don't trust that the organization
is looking out for them. Because it's not. It's just not.
And that's just how it is. It's fascinating. I mean it fascinating, in a really disturbing kind of way.

Lori: So this is an organization that is committed to ending
poverty, and it is within itself, fostering a lack of trust,
and a bureaucratic structure, where people as you
have said are in a golden cage, are being paid a lot of
money, they want to stay there, and at the same time
it's completely imprisoning. Is that right?

Interviewee: You've got a lack of accountability and you've got all
of the systems in place to force accountability because
there's no trust. So that detracts time and energy from
doing work because you're always doing reporting or
going to meetings and there's so much compliance.

If you are part of an organization where there is no room
for advancement and there is no trust because people are
competing for the attention of those above (managing up)
because there are so few opportunities, you may be a brilliant
manager and deeply committed to your staff, but I can easily
imagine you becoming demoralized because of the need to
cover your ass, and manage egos and politics above you, to
the point where you are unable to provide the support to your
staff, because no one above you cares. I can also imagine staff
being demoralized and frustrated and subsequently angry.
Maybe even with you. It's a no-win for everyone, and a good
example of how dysfunctional systems can impact managing. It is also a perfect example of recreating exactly what this
institution is working against: raising people out of poverty. If

the mission was reflected within the organization, there would be some form of stability, equity, and care for those "below," instead of the existing institutionalized hierarchy and ongoing divides between permanent/contract staff, lack of ability to contribute to decision-making, and lack of trust. Maybe those served might be asked what they think the problems and the solutions might be, and then the organization could base their plans on or incorporate those ideas.

4.6 Summary

Managing is a complex job involving systems, structures, policies, functions, and people that relate to one another for better and for worse. You have to keep your eye(s) on all of them and you have to prioritize the people/things that are going to seek out or attract your attention, often multiple times a day. You may have to give up the hands-on work that you loved, and/or you may be excited about learning new things and taking on new responsibilities. An increased salary may be much needed. Being conscious, at least of some of the internal and external responsibilities involved in taking the decision to move to a management role, is a good place to start. Because as a manager, you are going to impact people's lives. You may not think about it in the same way as impacting the lives of the people whom the organization serves, and in many ways it isn't. You and your team are working, are being paid, and, unless you are in a residential or humanitarian setting, get to leave and go home every night. Those being served by the organization continue to live with their concerns, lack of safety, need for a job, and so on. They don't get to leave it behind and pick it up again the next day. But you *are* going to impact the lives of your team and those around you. I think it's helpful to keep that in mind, knowing you will be a role model.

Managing in this way is not a recipe for an organizational free-for-all; I would argue that the people working in nonprofit organizations most often work hard and want to do a good job. They want their programs to succeed, they want to reach the mission. They also want recognition (including financial recognition) when they have done well, and they would like at least some consistency in their workplace and their managers. This is not so different than people in general; my experience is that people want to do a good job, be it parenting, working, or dieting.

As managers, our job includes recognizing all of these things in ourselves, our staff, and our systems, and acting in ways that nurture these innate motivations, and/or help those who are not able to do their jobs to move to somewhere where their skills and motivations can help them be successful. And to accept that a person's ability to manage is not solely the responsibility of managers; even the best manager in a bad system may not be able to participate in workplace relationships if those above that person are not amenable to reflection and change.

There are people who for many reasons should not be part of nonprofit organizations because they are not a good fit. If someone on your team is saying something or doing their job in a way that you would consider outside the accepted norm, it is your job to listen and to ask questions about why the person thinks the way they do. Through that, hopefully, you will gain some understanding and will be able to formulate a way to work with what you are hearing to determine a way forward. If the person you are managing is repeatedly playing basketball on a cricket pitch and you have explained cricket to them, they have seen other team members playing, and they have a position to play, they will likely start playing cricket, or they will need to look for a basketball court and team somewhere else. (A sports metaphor! I am utterly pleased with myself.)

But what if the "badness of fit" is above you? Wait! Why, in fact I have *another* sports analogy! It concerns team owners and problems down the line, and has been written about by Jeb Lund in *Rolling Stone* (2014) and David Zirin in *Bad Sports: How Owners Are Ruining the Games We Love* (2010), citing issues of team failure due to the firing of coaches, bad managers, Ponzi schemes, greed, inequity in player salaries, regular changes in players, forcing poor draft picks, making bad trades, and plain old greed. If the owner sees the team as a means to an end, whether that end is money or power or influence, that person may run the operations of the team to garner wealth, power, or influence. Even if it means that, like the NY Knicks, they have won only one playoff series since 2000. For many owners, it's no longer about the love of the game, or the fans (unless they are forking over hundreds of dollars for a ticket), or the athletes, it's about money in their pocket or who they can invite to sit in their private box. The owner expects there to be a team when, at the top, there is no team. Hence, we have the Cincinnati Bengals with a record of 145-222-1 since 1991 (Lund, 2014). The owner calls the shots, and coaches, managers, and players leave. Teams lose. Sometimes, you just have to walk away—and that's easier said than done if you are the primary breadwinner.

I am so proud of myself. Since there are so few women writing books on management and I'm thinking that men will be hesitant to pick up this book because it is written by a woman (your loss, for sure), please know that it includes examples from SPORTS!

Now that I have exhausted my athletic analogy abilities, we are going to wrap up the management chapter, and figure out how to put mission, process, and managing together. Just turn the page.

Chapter V

Linking Managing, Mission, and Process

In short, you can't let the deadline define the mission. The mission has to define the duration.

Richard Holbrooke

Kempster, 1998

... how you get the best out of your people, you take care of your people, is one of the roles of management that is really important. I think a lot of times ... if you get too mission-focused, you forget that your organization is about more than the mission, it's about your people and your mission. It's about how you get people to come together around this idea that you can accomplish this. Whether it's the board of directors, the executive director, or any level of management, depending on the size of the organization, you need to be able to motivate and listen to your team, provide a direction, and bring people together around that. And I don't know if you can say that reviewing budgets and approving travel is about being a manager, but [it's about] the people underneath. If you're a good manager, you don't care about what the people above you say, it's about what the people below you say. (Interviewee, 2016)

5.1 Managing As Mission

At this point, you have thought about the history of "mission" and what that means regarding the creation and implementation of your organization's mission, and have considered the roles of fear and hope in achieving the mission. You have thought about process, the "how" of getting to the mission and the idea that the how is undergirded by values, behaviors, relationships, trust, uncertainty, and change. You have considered the ways in which an organization can get to an agreed-upon process (confusion to understanding) through the creation of a Values Statement, Code of Ethics, Process Statement and looking at the spaces in between to manifest the kinds of relationships that make for a world we want to see within the constructs of the workplace. You then reflected on management and managing, have asked yourself if you want to manage, and thought about issues of power, authority, and control, as well as your relationship to hierarchy, structures, systems, and people. This is the chapter where we put all of this together and see what it can look like in practice (Figure 5.1).

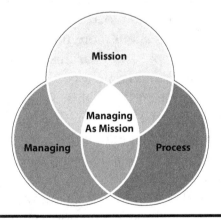

Figure 5.1 Managing As Mission.

Previously, I listed managing styles, but I don't want to give the impression that a manager is one thing and only one thing—it's like reducing a person to one trait like being a lefty. A person is much more than left-handed, although it is a defining characteristic and leads to doing things in a certain way. Different managing styles may be needed for different workplaces, tasks, individuals. And although no one is one thing all the time, an individual's personality does impact how they manage, tilting them more toward one style than another. Because of this, I thought it might be fun to look at a couple of these styles and project out, to determine what a world might look like if it was governed/led by people using one specific style. I'm going to describe a style; I'd like you to read it, then think about the world if it were led and managed by people using that style. There is even some space below each description for you to make notes, and so you can't see what *I'm* thinking. And after you are done, then you can read my ideas and we can compare notes.

Let's start with Directive.

A Directive manager is described as a person who is clear about what they see needing to be done, defines expectations, sets rules, and gives directions. In a less favorable light, directive managing can manifest as coercive, controlling,

Jot your notes.

demanding compliance, and a "do as I tell you" methodology enforced by threats. How might this world look?

A directively managed world would probably look a lot like basic training in the army. There would be a centralized authority that made the rules and dictated what needed to be done and how to do it. From growing crops to creating microchips, things would be done in specific ways, leading to a lot of proscribed ways of functioning and regulations for everything in life. Maybe down to brushing your teeth. Which would have the potential of restricting creative or inventive thought, and there would be people who would not fit in and would want to rebel—but as in basic training, you would conform or you would go AWOL and be court-martialed and jailed. Or if you learned great survival skills you might make it in the desert or the woods, but what fun would that be long term? Unless there were others like you, and now we have a dystopian young adult novel so let's leave it there.

You most likely would not have a lot of close relationships with those outside of your group, whether you were the director or the directee, and would probably better relate to people who are "on your level" or doing what you do—either because there is not a lot of room for movement up, or because you have been indoctrinated to maintain your place in the world. Or both. You might have a great deal of trust in those providing direction if the person/system providing direction is transparent and provides what you need to live your life. Or you might become apathetic and depressed. You might live in a state of fear, of being threatened by others if you don't stick with the program. And even if you have good ideas, they may never be heard because "it's not the way we do things here."

5.1.1 Affiliative

How about an Affiliative manager, one who is great at team-building, creating trust, connecting people, raising morale, providing positive and minimizing negative feedback, and is

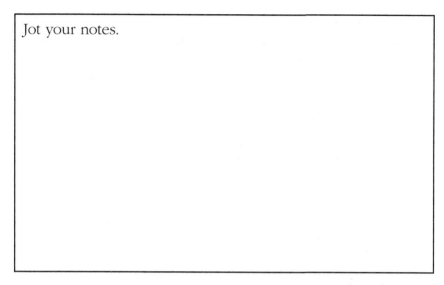

less likely to want to deal with problems and conflict? What might a world look like if it ran on an affiliative model?

Take a couple of minutes, jot notes in the space.

Initially, this sounds great. People would be lifted up, happiness and getting along would be the goal, people would feel linked to one another and, hopefully, to the environment. Doors to houses would remain unlocked because people would trust one another. In the affiliative world, people would be loyal to the person in charge because everyone would get an award, and who doesn't want an award? Even if you are not doing a great job, you are still part of the team and can get the same award as everyone else. And if everyone is the same, if all get awards, there shouldn't be conflict, right?

Maybe after multiple millennia, if we haven't completely mucked up the planet and destroyed ourselves, we might not engage in the kinds of behaviors, internal or external, that lead to conflict. The dilemma is that as of now we are all human and, although we are made from the same stuff as the Dalai Lama, most of us (myself included) are going to do things that others don't like or vice versa. Maybe not pull their weight because they'll get the award anyway. Which could easily lead to conflict.

If we have not learned how to successfully navigate conflict and there is a rub, a twinge of internal discomfort triggered by someone's actions (or our own internal process: I want donuts! Donuts will increase the pounds. I WANT DONUTS! NO DONUTS!), we may not be prepared to deal with the situation, denying or repressing the conflicting feeling. Which can lead to inertia: a world where things don't change because people cannot deal with differences of opinion. Or we might have *Fight Club*, where people knock the stuffing out of each other and then shake hands and nobody talks about it because the first rule of Fight Club is … you do not talk about Fight Club! I can see a world of frustrated people because problems don't get solved.

5.1.2 Walking Around

How about management by walking around? This was a fundamental modality at Hewlett-Packard, where both Hewlett and Packard, in an informal way, walked around the company randomly asking questions and getting ideas. What would a world look like where, instead of people in their office sending emails to people 10 feet from them, they got up and walked around and talked to everyone at least part of the time, asked questions, listened, and then as much as possible, attempted to respond to needs and take on ideas?

Jot your notes.

As social beings, humans form relationships. Studies show that if there are positive relationships with coworkers and supervisors, job performance increases (Amjad et al., 2015). A world reflective of managing by walking around implies that there is an accepted structure, and that in contrast to telling people what to do and how to do it, there is a genuine interest on the part of those who are in charge in knowing about how things are working in the day-to-day of one's life, and what people think about the best ways forward for the community and world. Although there is a structure, due to an uncoupling from hierarchy there is less of a gap between those in charge and everyone else. In a world created by walking around, political leaders would regularly hold town hall meetings, attend events like pancake breakfasts, go to workplaces and schools, and actually listen to their constituents. It is not unlike U.S. democracy (at its best), where politicians attend meetings to "take the pulse" of their home districts. It is different in that in the world, leaders in democracies are elected, and in corporations, the founder/owner/CEO is not (in most cases) elected and gets a larger share of the wealth than those being asked for their opinions. (Maybe *not* so different from democratic politics …) And it works when what people say is acted upon by those asking the questions. People would probably feel valued, they would think critically, barriers would be lessened between people. I'm sure there are downsides in this world, the implication is that control and compensation remain the same, but it seems there would be a better chance of civic participation if people felt valued, could see change being made based on their ideas, and then felt empowered to do more.

I purposefully did not use either command or control because that would have been too easy for you—and for me. You paid good money for this book, and I've been asking you to also do some of the writing, which hardly seems fair. It's a change from what you might be used to when buying a book, but this is a book about change and I'm hoping that you'll stick with it, even with the exercises, all the way through.

You are getting the idea, right? That managing can enforce or reduce hierarchy. It can encourage new ideas or shut them down. Your team members are impacted by this. And that as managers, we are prone to one style or another based on experience, neural circuitry, values, and that style may or may not create an environment in which your team is most productive, is doing the best job they can do, or is reflective of a better world. And different team members respond to different ways of managing; some people are comfortable with direction, others do best when their manager is a sounding board for ideas.

It takes two to manage, the manager and the managee. If we think about creating a better world in the space in between manager and managee, we have made a deliberate decision to think and interact with team members in a different way. We are managing differently.

* * *

5.2 Determining the World Your Organization Wants, and Getting There through Managing

We've thought a lot about process, mission, and managing. We haven't thought so much about the specifics of the world you want to see, and for the rest of the chapter we'll determine how to figure that out, and how to get there through managing.

Getting to the world you want to see can take the form of a discussion that includes those served by the organization, the staff, and hopefully the board. It's big picture, visionary. It pulls in all the previous work you've done on values, ethics, process, and relationships, as well as your mission and vision. Staff might want to review these documents prior to the discussion.

This discussion has the potential to be both expansive and digressive, and your job as manager is to ensure that it comes back to the mission of the organization and what *that* means for the world you want to see. You'll need a facilitator and a note-taker, and the exercise will take from one to two hours.

Getting to the world the organization wants begins with a set of big-picture questions that can then be defined. Some of those questions might be

■ What would a person's life look like in the world we want?

■ What does the planet look like in the world we want?

■ What would relationships look like in the world we want?

You might want to think economically, socially, healthcare-wise, educationally, in terms of information, housing, nourishment, water, environment, and so on. I'd suggest that whoever is facilitating this discussion brainstorm possible questions with other staff. Or you might want to start with a set of principles like the Universal Declaration of Human Rights (UDHR) or the United Nations (UN) Sustainable Development Goals[*] and go from there. You can create a statement from the results of the conversation, or you can leave the answers in categorized lists based on your questions. Putting the world your organization wants into categories will provide easier access to that information for later exercises.

In the chapter on Process, we used the mission of Oxfam, *To create lasting solutions to poverty, hunger, and social injustice*, as an example. Let's use it here to build the bridge to managing.

Table 5.1 describes how the world we want plus our mission plus our process/values/ethics statements can lead to behaviors that inform managing. For ease, I'm again using the UDHR as the basis of the world I want to see.

---

[*] http://www.un.org/sustainabledevelopment/sustainable-development-goals/.

Table 5.1   Generating Possible Behaviors Toward Those Served by the Organization Based on the World We Want

The World We Want	Beliefs	Values	View of Those Served	Oxfam's Mission	Behaviors toward Those Served	Managing Behaviors
Is sustainable. Is equitable. Is just. People have rights, including enough food and other resources to flourish. Relationships between people are not conflict-free, but they are non-violent.	All people should be able to live lives of dignity that are free from want. People are equal. We need environmental sustainability if solutions are to be lasting. Violence does not help.	Equality. Respect. Compassion. Honesty. Justice. Optimism. Kindness. Trustworthiness.	The person in front of me has worth, abilities, knowledge, and strengths. The person has rights just as I do. The person has a right to respect.	Create lasting solutions to poverty, hunger, and social injustice.	Asking questions to better understand problems and gather ideas for sustainable solutions. Inclusion in problem-solving, which can lead to sustainability. Exchange of information. Smiling. Eye contact.*	

If the world we want is just, equitable, sustainable, and non-violent, and people have rights, then we believe that people's rights should be honored including that they have inherent dignity and worth. Values then form from those beliefs, and those values inform the ways in which we see the people with whom the organization works. All of this is then filtered through the mission, which provides a lens to determine how those working inside the organization relate to those outside of the organization.

You'll notice that Managing Behaviors is blank. It's ok, we're not there yet! If you have ideas, please put them in, don't wait for me, and we can see in a bit whether your current ideas line up with your ideas later in the chapter. As described in the Process chapter, there may need to be a review of the mission statement at this point to determine if the components of the mission, for example, "those in need," are actually how you want to frame those served by your organization. It may be, but a discussion of the values and behaviors that can come from a larger framing might change the mission, how the work is done, and maybe even the vision statement.

You're doing great. Now that we have all that information, what do we do with it, and what does it have to do with managing?

5.3 Managing As Mission: How It Happens

Now is your turn to ask me, "Now that I have done all of this work, tell me, what is my specific role if I'm managing as mission? How do I make the world better through managing my team and really, isn't this a big burden to put on my shoulders? I have to be willing to revise my view of the whole idea of mission, to be willing to change, to listen, to uphold and possibly suggest changes to the mission, co-create values and ethics, be sure people know the process of the organization, have integrity, be responsible and transparent, create charts and diagrams, look at relationships, consider 'Thou,' and do all of this while trying to do my job?"

And I answer: "Yes. Yes you do. But you don't have to do it all at once. It takes time and practice."

And you ask: "Well what about those I am managing? Do they have to do all of this, too?"

And I respond: "Yes. If you set the tone, they will. Or, as in *Field of Dreams*, 'If you build it, they will come'" (sports analogy 3, or movie reference? You decide).

And you say: "What if my organization doesn't care about these things and doesn't want to engage in this kind of thinking?"

And I say: "Then you have to make a decision. If you've done everything you can think of to make the kinds of changed described in this book with no success, then you know something. You know that change is not going to happen, and you need to decide whether to stay and create as much of a safe space for your team to do their work or, if your situation allows, to look for another job where the fit is better."

Managing can be as simple as telling someone what to do. But the actualities, the day-to-day of managing should be more nuanced, and that's what differentiates an ok manager (or a terrible one) from a great one, and either reinforces or changes the status quo. Traditionally, one's role as manager is to ensure the work gets done so the mission is met. If our mission and our process are one in the same, we need to figure out what that means for *you* managing. Because most of us have not had formal training in managing, or have been told that managing is about command and control or, if we come from a cultural group that is more top-down, we will have ideas about how to do our jobs and achieve mission, based on our experience. Which could be good or not so good.

But, you might ask, aren't we then turning our nonprofits into staff coddling services? Where first-world people benefit from what is supposed to go to those served by the organization? Or where people work in irresponsible ways? Or don't work because everything is discussed and nothing gets done?

No.

At least in my lifetime, most of the people in the world are going to have to engage in work of some kind, and many of us are going to do that work as part of a company or organization. Food needs to be grown. Dwellings need to be built. Technology needs to be serviced. Structures and processes need to be organized and managed. People need incomes to buy the food, the structures, and maybe even the technology. So why not work to change the world through something that already exists?

As a manager in an organization, you are modeling ways of getting to the mission, as reflected in the process of how the work gets done and how the organization operates, to everyone around you. If, as a manager, I am talking negatively about a team member with another team member, I am modeling. If my door is closed for most of the day, I am modeling. If my behavior is unpredictable from day to day, I am modeling. People are much more observant than you might think, and the old adage "don't do as I do, do as I say" came from somewhere.

If we manage as mission, we are treating staff based on the world we want and so often in nonprofits, staff are treated in ways that we would NEVER treat those served by the organization. Comp time instead of overtime pay. Being surprised or embarrassed in meetings. No cost of living raises due to tight budgets. Staff being groped by donors at events. Expectations that people will go above and beyond because they are mission-driven. Not consulted when planning or making change. True that people working in nonprofit organizations, most of the time, are in at least slightly better situations than those being served; I will not argue that point. The reason to treat staff as they want to be treated (within the scope of the job, of course), is very simple. It shows respect and lets staff know that you are paying attention to their individual worth and dignity. And in turn, they will understand that the same behaviors are expected of them because they have helped in creating that expectation through the processes described previously—it's sustainable. Indeed if your team has the experience of being supported, heard, participating, they will treat those with whom the organization works in the same way ... and you know the next line (if I've done my job) ... leading to the world we want.

If the world I want to see is the one described by the UDHR, and the UN Charter, it follows that every individual, including children, has dignity, worth, and rights. Men and women are equal, justice is the same for all based on rule of law, diversity is celebrated, there is freedom of speech and belief and responsible production and consumption. If these are the beliefs and values through which I look at my organization's mission, I have to think about each of these and how I and the organization need to function to ensure these are reflected in my managing.

The following questions provide a way to think about getting to managing as mission to achieve the world *I* want to see. Yours may be the same or different, but the process is essentially the same.

- What would it mean to lift up the worth, dignity, and rights of staff?
- To treat all people equally in the workplace?
- To ensure justice is the same for all based on rule of law?
- To embrace and grow from diversity?
- To ensure freedom of speech and belief?
- To reach the mission?
- To operate in a transparent manner?
- To create methods for responsible production and consumption?

Worth, dignity, rights, equality, justice, diversity, free speech and belief, mission, transparency, responsible production and consumption. Then, the next step is to determine how you think about and implement these ideas. This can be done fairly quickly; in Table 5.2, I have delineated the ideas I want to see and have noted how I think about the ideas/values and how they relate to staff.

If you believe that individuals in the larger world have worth, then the same would apply to those on your team. How would that belief/value translate to managing them? If they have rights and dignity? Column one in Table 5.2 is a delineation of the ideas within the world we want—when you do this, items in this column will come directly from your discussion on the world you want. Column two is a list of the beliefs and values within the world we want. Column three is a view of the team or staff, based on the ideas in columns one and two; for example, if the world we want includes dignity, then people on my team or on staff are worthy of respect. In column three, I ask myself as a manager, "If staff are worthy of respect, how do I show that respect?" and in column four, I think about managing behaviors that could convey respect to my team and other staff. I'm not asking you to write this time, just to read and think.

These are ideas for ways of behaving toward and working with your team, and others in the organization, to create a better world right inside your organization; however, this is not an exhaustive list and comes out of the world I want to see.

This exercise can be done by managers individually, or as a group. It can also be used to help new managers figure out how they can build working relationships with staff so that mission and process become one. If it's to be successful, the organization as a whole has to have decided on a Values Statement and the world they want to see, so that everything else can flow from that.

In your team discussion of getting to the world you want, asking, not telling, is primary. Listening must accompany asking, and is inherent in I-Thou. And because I-Thou implies a mutuality, your team needs to listen to one another, as well as

Table 5.2 Generating Possible Managing Behaviors Based on the World We Want

The World We Want	Beliefs/Values the Organization Wants to See	My View of those on My Team/in My Organization	Questions to Ask as a Manager	Possible Managing Behaviors
Is sustainable. Is equitable. Is just. People have rights, including enough food and other resources to flourish.	Worth.	Staff have value. Staff bring experience.	How do I let my staff know that I see their value and experience?	Acknowledge that your staff exists: Say hello, ask how they are doing. Walk around and ask questions. Give positive and constructive feedback. Celebrate successes/job well done.
	Dignity.	Worthy of respect. People believe in their self-worth.	How do I show respect to my staff?	Listen. Honor what people bring to the workplace. Talk honestly about performance.
Relationships between people are not conflict-free, but they are non-violent.	Rights.	Staff have human rights. Staff have rights within the law.	How are human rights incorporated into work with my staff?	Hang the UDHR in the office. Discuss a right in each team meeting. Ask what rights mean in their work with constituents.

(Continued)

Table 5.2 (Continued)   Generating Possible Managing Behaviors Based on the World We Want

The World We Want	Beliefs/Values the Organization Wants to See	My View of those on My Team/in My Organization	Questions to Ask as a Manager	Possible Managing Behaviors
	Mission.	Staff are working to meet a goal.	How does my staff know about the mission? Have they had a hand in creating it? Can they recite it? What does it mean to them? How are they working to meet it?	Post the mission all over the organization. Discuss the mission in team meetings. Do the values exercise. Ask what success looks like to each of them. Ask how they see getting there. Meeting deadlines.
	Transparency.	Staff should know how the org works. Staff need to be clear about roles and responsibilities. Staff need to be kept apprised of financial matters.	What are the parameters of transparency? How do I relay information to staff? Do I talk about myself? Do I talk about others?	Determine what people know and what they want/need to know. Ensure clear job descriptions, values, and ethics. Determine how to deliver messages to staff. You will be told the truth about your performance. Never talk about one staff person to another staff person. Your personal problems are yours. Your work problems are yours.

(Continued)

Table 5.2 (Continued) Generating Possible Managing Behaviors Based on the World We Want

The World We Want	Beliefs/Values the Organization Wants to See	My View of those on My Team/in My Organization	Questions to Ask as a Manager	Possible Managing Behaviors
				Create a system to allow staff to see overall spending and income. Everyone is getting the same structure/systems/policies/processes messages.
	Equality and justice.	All of us are operating under the same strictures.	Am I coming from a place where I see staff as unique individuals, and at the same time ensure equal application of policies and legal frameworks?	Be clear about policies, laws. Apply all policies equally. Ensure equal pay for equal work.
	Diversity.	We are different from one another, yet we all have a "piece of the truth" and are working toward the same goal.	How do I think about hiring staff? Is my team reflective of the population served? How do I elicit and synthesize different ways of knowing/experience? How do we as practitioners or finance or development relate to other departments?	Hiring is based on reflecting the mission. Have team discussions. Ask questions and ensure as many people as possible participate. Be interested in responses. Synthesize to ensure clarity. Review and work to improve working relationships between my team and other teams/departments. Creation of a safe space for all staff.

(Continued)

Table 5.2 (Continued) Generating Possible Managing Behaviors Based on the World We Want

The World We Want	Beliefs/Values the Organization Wants to See	My View of those on My Team/in My Organization	Questions to Ask as a Manager	Possible Managing Behaviors
	Freedom of speech and belief	Everyone has a right to believe and say what they want.	What are the parameters for speech based on the values, ethics, mission, and job descriptions of all staff?	With team, and using values and ethics, establish guidance around speech. Beliefs need to resonate with values, ethics, and mission. Good facilitation can ensure discussions stay on topic.
	Sustainable production and consumption.	Funding/resources. Environment.	Are my staff taking vacation? Are they working long hours? Do they take breaks? Do we have the financial resources to do our jobs well? Is the environment conducive to work? Is there recycling? And so on.	Ensure staff are working reasonable hours and are taking vacations. Put out recycling bins.

you listening to them (and they need to listen to you, too, but mind yourself, let them do most of the talking). It is a way to get to a unified, agreed-upon way of being, or culture, within your team.

Does I-Thou allow for structure? I would argue that it does, and it's another way to unlink structure from hierarchy, because it builds trust. Your role is manager, and that should be clear from your job description. You are not a doormat, nor should you be a bully. Managing is about understanding roles and responsibilities, systems, and structures, and working with each person to fulfill their role—do their job—in relation to one another and the people served by the organization. Good job descriptions really help. People are responsible for their actions and behaviors, including, and especially, those with a certain amount of authority as part of their job description. You are engaging in/modeling behaviors that can create a world that you and your team/organization want to see, and through those behaviors, staff know whether you are authentically committed to a new way of doing things, and whether to trust you (or not).

If you decide to undertake any of these exercises, you need to make an agreement with yourself that you will follow through on ideas that come out of the discussions. If you don't, the experience of your team will be one of "doing harm." The biggest single casualty of not following through will be trust, and without trust there is little basis for working together. As a person who is managing, creating a sense of trust is the most important thing you can do with your team. Trust is built in the space in between two or more people, and if it is to be a living trust, it is mutual—you have to trust your team, and your team has to trust you. The same is true for other departments, donors, and the people served by the organization, and it is especially important when there is difficult news to be delivered.

5.4 Managing As Mission: Getting it Right from the Start

Picture a scenario where you are really looking forward to going to a new place, somewhere you have never been before. You've planned the best you can, have maps and a guide-book, think you have a pretty good idea of how to get there, have talked with people about their experiences traveling to the place you are going; you've even packed snacks in case the food is not exactly to your liking. You arrive at your destination and, although you have a working knowledge of the language, there are phrases you don't understand at all. Cars are riding on the opposite side of the road, and the stick shift, along with the steering wheel, is on the opposite side of the vehicle. Everyone seems to know where they are going, people are laughing, talking to one another while walking. The route you were going to take to your lodgings has been changed due to construction, and you have not planned an alternate route. When you finally get to your accommodation, you are given a room, and you finally have a chance to take a breath.

This is often how a new staff person will feel starting their job. Policies may be different. The specifics of the mission will have changed from their last job. There is a different office setup, as well as different technology systems. Everyone seems to know everyone else and seems to be doing their job with ease.

Managing as mission starts at the first meeting (actually, it starts with the first interview so the person interviewing is clear about the organizational culture, ensuring goodness of fit) with a new staff person. If, as manager, you are clear about the inherent worth, dignity, and rights of all people, you are going to want to arrange your introductions and orientation so that this is demonstrated, and a good place to start is with the idea that this is going to be an I-Thou meeting, and then make an offer of tea, coffee, or another beverage (but not a *drink* drink—this is work).

When you orient new staff, do you welcome them to the organization and introduce them to the team? Have you thought about what is important for them to know? Do you describe the organization and its policies, structures, values? Review their job responsibilities? Show them their desk/cube/office/chair? Have you set up a first-couple-of-weeks' schedule? Let them know that they can talk to you whenever they need information? Ask if they have questions?

All of these things can be helpful; your job as their manager is to make sure (as much as is in your control—the staff person has to want to do a good job, be part of a team, and hopefully you have determined this prior to asking them to come to work for your organization) that they have the best possible start, know and understand their job responsibilities and the culture of the organization, feel like they belong, and know that you are glad they are on board.

In addition to the previous considerations, it's helpful to lay out expectations that go beyond the "mechanicals" of the job description (tasks, reporting, work hours, etc.). When I bring on new staff, we usually have a conversation that goes something like this:

> Now that we're done with the preliminary part of the orientation, I'd like you to know what my expectations of you are, and then to hear what your expectations are of me in your new role. These are my expectations:
>
> - That you hold the mission paramount, and that the way you work is reflective of the mission (and what that means)
> - That there is respect for those with whom we are working
> - That you work hard *and* smart
> - That you ask questions
> - That you are a team player

- That you have a sense of humor
- And that there are no surprises

And then I do some explaining of the expectations. Holding the mission and working as a way of reflecting the mission is what we've been discussing for the past 150+ pages. Working hard is clear; what I always include is that I expect people to work, as much as possible, within their allotted hours per week and that they take their vacation days. ALL of them. Remember, burnout is no one's friend.

Working smart means planning, consulting, strategizing, implementing, and measuring to determine results. It means prioritizing; looking at what needs to be done and what can wait; and contributing ideas and wrestling with ideas that are different from yours without dismissing them out of hand. Being a team player means collaboration, solving problems, figuring out how to work together, supporting one another. And if there are differences, trying to work them out before coming to me.

Having a sense of humor is never about laughing "at" someone unless it is laughing at yourself. It's more about keeping a sense of perspective regarding work and about laughing together—which can unite us as humans.

And finally, that there are no surprises. I never want to walk into a meeting to find out that something has been done or said without me, as your manager, knowing. Nor would I expect that this would make you jump for joy if the situation were reversed. If there is a problem, or if something goes wrong (or right), I want to know, then we can celebrate it or fix it. If there is trust and regular communication in the working relationship, surprises are much less likely to happen. And then there is Human Resources if there are working relationship issues you feel cannot be overcome through us talking together.

Then I ask, "What are your expectations of me as a supervisor?" In the typical power relationship, newly hired staff are expecting to be told how they should do their jobs, when to report in, when to go home. They're not often asked what *they* expect. This is a signal to the person that in *this* job there will be dialogue—actually, that it will be expected. Hopefully, they get the message that this is a work relationship in the best interest of something bigger than any one person, not a power struggle. Through an orientation like this, you have established that they were hired for their abilities to contribute as well as their skills to do the work, that they have worth and dignity, that there are policies and legalities by which everyone must abide.

It's completely possible to do this without ever ceding your role as manager; in fact, as described previously, if you are a manager who is holding the mission and processes first, you won't often have to exercise your authority. And that is a wonderful thing for you, for the staff, and for the mission; it sets the tone for how the work will get done. Setting the tone in that first meeting lets staff know a number of things:

■ That you see the mission and how you get to the mission as one in the same
■ That you respect them
■ That you hired them for their ability to do the job
■ That you are transparent
■ That you are clear about boundaries and what is acceptable in the workplace

Because your place of work is just that—a place of work. It's not home, it's not a friend's house. You have to hold and embody the mission and the process not just for yourself, but for others, too, and they then need to hold and embody the mission and the process for those with whom the organization works. The way you conduct yourself is the example of your respect or lack of respect for the mission and how to get there—and that is why we do this work, right?

5.5 Ongoing Managing As Mission

Next are some ideas on actually carrying out the behaviors listed to get to Managing As Mission. I will not cover all of them because these are my ideas, and you need to develop your own with your team, and also because if I talked in-depth about each one, we would never get to the end of this book.

5.5.1 Worth

5.5.1.1 Give Positive and Constructive Feedback

If someone is doing well at their job, do you let them know? A general "great job" is good; however, grounding the positive comment in specific actions or interventions makes the feedback much more real, and provides specifics on what is working well. If I say in passing, "Hey Megan, you did a great job in the meeting yesterday," Megan will probably feel good. She may know what intervention I am referring to, but there's no guarantee. If I say in passing, or better yet in a one-to-one meeting, "Megan, your inputs during yesterday's meeting, particularly the examples on how we might advocate for the end of child marriage, were really helpful. Which ones do you think had the most relevance for the staff?" I have let her know that she's done a good job, highlighted the area in which she did a good job, and considered how she thinks this good work might be carried forward. Megan leaves empowered, feels recognized both individually and as part of the team, thinks about her possible impact on others, and has contributed to the greater mission. She knows she's moving in the right direction, and a number of the factors that lead to happy staff have been incorporated into the feedback.

If you are not comfortable with this approach, write out a script for yourself. A list of bullet points. Practice. It will come more naturally as you do it, and your staff will appreciate it.

When giving constructive feedback—and I do mean constructive, helping your team to do their jobs more effectively—you might want to approach the issue of concern with questions. If you see mission and process as the same, you are probably not going to want to say, "*Wow, did you mess up in that meeting!*," or the famous "*Let's think about how we can do this better next time.*" You know your team, and thinking about how they might want to be approached when there's a problem will be helpful to you and to your team member. Does the person embarrass easily? Are they hard on themselves when they make mistakes? Do they have a hard time acknowledging errors? Asking a general question and then narrowing down can be helpful. You might start with, "So how do you think yesterday's meeting went?" and see what they say. Do they bring up the concern? If yes, I'd ask what they might have done differently to both get an idea of their thinking and about how it might be most successfully addressed. If they don't mention the concern, you are going to have to take a more direct route, maybe by saying, "There was a part of the meeting yesterday that didn't go as usual" (then describe it)—"what did you think about it?" This strategy allows you to problem-solve with them which, again, shows respect and your valuing of them as part of your staff.

5.5.2 Dignity

5.5.2.1 Be Consistent and Expect Consistency, Be Truthful and Expect Truthfulness

(OK, so I am addressing two ideas within dignity, even though my intention was to only address one in each category—and ironically, I am talking about consistency and am being inconsistent with what I wrote earlier about only addressing one behavior in each. Happens to all of us. It's recognizing it and acting on it that counts. That said, I'm going ahead with my inconsistency.)

Trust is based on honesty and consistency. What does this mean for dignity? Let's take consistency first. Think about what you would want in a manager. Would you want to work under someone who is moody, who is expansive and inclusive on some days and makes unilateral decisions on others? Who schedules then cancels meetings? Who doesn't tell you that they are going on vacation? I didn't think so. I surely wouldn't. It demonstrates a lack of respect for the other, and a lack of commitment to the work.

As a manager, you want to check yourself before you go into work. Did you argue with your partner this morning? Was the train/subway/bus/car delayed causing frustration? If yes, can you ask yourself whether you are ready to do your job, or if you need just a few minutes to pull yourself together to work in a way that is consistent with how you worked yesterday? I'm not talking about coming to work after a catastrophe like a death or some other tragedy. You will need time off after that; however, the way you handle things may not be the way others handle them, so it's important not to project your way onto others. If you are consistent in your behaviors, and those behaviors include arrogance, competition, or demeaning or undermining others, I know you probably haven't gotten this far in the book so I'm not going to say more. Being consistent in your presentation—as much as possible—is hugely helpful to all; it lets people know that you respect them enough to modify your own behavior in the interest of them getting their work done.

Consistency is about setting patterns that create order. Regular meetings with staff, with agendas, can do a number of things. If you have a set time to meet with each staff member, that staff member knows that every week (or two weeks or as often as agreed) they have a place to talk out problems, share successes, explore ideas, get feedback, and so on. It's an escape valve, a safe place. Consistency also includes living up to your word. If you have a meeting and you have to cancel the meeting whether five minutes before or the day before, giving a bit of explanation can be helpful—unless the matter is personal to you or someone else—then you can just say "The matter is personal to me" (or someone else), and if you've been consistent, chances are your staff will take that at face value, and internally they will know that the same will apply to them in another circumstance.

Honesty is a fantastic concept; the key in honesty is the behaviors associated with it. If you are in a meeting and someone makes a suggestion that has been tried before multiple times, you will want to first consider whether the person is new, or whether they have been presenting the same idea even after it has been tried and shown not to work. You might do a number of things. You could roll your eyes, blow out your breath and say, "Are you bringing this up again? We've tried that before multiple times and it didn't work. Next?" You could remain silent and let someone else in the group address it. You might ask to speak with the person after the meeting. Or you might ask why they have brought it up again. So many possibilities!

I always try diligently to ensure that people are not humiliated in public—this is one of the surest ways to negate the inherent dignity of another—even if they have overstepped, unless they have overstepped to the point where they are hurting another person or impacting the mission. Then, as manager your job is to intervene to stop the behavior in a way that reduces, not exacerbates, the tension. If the organization has created a values and ethics statement along with some of the other exercises suggested in this book, chances are you won't ever get to this point, and if you do, you have agreed-upon parameters to fall back on.

How honest should you be with staff? I use the "need to know" rule. Before I talk about something, I ask myself, "does this person need to know this to do their job?" If the answer is yes, then we talk about it. If no, then we don't. And please don't talk about your staff with others of your staff. It is one of the quickest ways to create a hostile environment and undermine trust. If you have issues with staff and you don't know what to do, talk to *your* manager and figure it out.

5.5.3 Rights

5.5.3.1 Knowing Your Human Rights

In the nonprofit world, almost all of our work is based on the idea that each of us has rights because we are human and we exist on this planet. Many of the rights cited in the UDHR have been broken down into sections in the previous table on Worth, Dignity, Equality. The thing is that many people don't have any idea about human rights and what those rights are.

When I ran a youth health center in the U.S., I framed a copy of the Convention on the Rights of the Child, and hung it on my office wall. It sent a message to me every time I looked at it, and it set the tone for staff knowing I prioritized this. You might want to provide a copy of the Universal Declaration to all staff, or review one of the rights in a team meeting, asking how staff see it as applying to both those served by the organization and the organization itself. This can feed directly into your values and ethics discussions.

5.5.4 Mission

What does success look like to each team member, and how do they see getting there?

One of the questions I asked during interviews for this book was, "Based on your organization's mission, what did success look like, and how do you see your organization getting there?" And there were many interesting answers, most of which focused on merged ends/means ideas. One interviewee said:

> [success looked like] the community self-organizing assisted by staff, there was some instruction, there was some on-the-job training, there was some making connections or developing relationships with employers or other service providers in education or whatever, so all of those kinds of things figured in

in terms of the service delivery ... For example the childcare component, or maintenance of the facilities, the work being done was being done by people training to do the work either there or elsewhere. The community development was the means and the outcome in a sense. *(Interviewee, 2016)*

Another interviewee said,

We want all communities to recognize that they can choose their own future. They don't have to choose any particular paradigm that is imposed on them or imported from somewhere else ... it's everyone coming together. *(Interviewee, 2016)*

A third interviewee said,

All of this is based on the premise, and this is what I find powerful, countries should lead their own work and their own development. That everyone has had expertise because they've had experiences doing things, whatever those things are, like service delivery, and what not, these ministries are serving their own clients and populations and they have experience in doing this and if these can be identified and captured and shared within their institutions and across states and countries or provinces and even from that country to another country, that that will help reach the goals and objectives ... Everyone is seen as an expert so it turns the traditional idea of international technical assistance on its head. *(Interviewee, 2016)*

Another interviewee said,

I think success to me based on the mission, really looks like some pretty concrete examples. So today we

took a trip to [XXX]. And when I saw a [child] on the
trip fall down and skin their knee, one of their class-
mates came over and asked if they needed any water.
Because the kids are trained that when they see a child
being hurt, to ask if there's something they can do to
improve that child's situation. So as a four-year-old they
do things that are in their control. So can I get you
some water? Can I get you an ice pack? And so seeing
that kindness that they're taught by their teachers lived
in practice in a real-life setting speaks to the work that
we're trying to do, and how that will carry with them
into their years after their time at the school.
(Interviewee, 2016)

One of the things that strikes me about all of these is
the implication that there is an organically unfolding way of
getting to the mission, in addition to a strategic plan, which
includes a willingness to incorporate new ideas and thinking.
In many organizations, the means to success/mission have
already been established. What happens when new data or
theories emerge either within or outside the organization? As a
manager, what is your role in this?

If one of your team has an idea about how to do work better or more effectively or by bringing in a new modality for
program work, you have a number of choices. If you have created an environment, a culture, where ideas and learning are
valued and encouraged, then there may already be a mechanism for discussion and experimentation or incorporation. You
might have the team member with the idea vet it with other
members of the team after discussing it with you. This way
the idea can be refined, honed, and a plan for implementation
can be developed. If there is an atmosphere of critical thought,
other staff will then participate in the discussion to ensure that
the best program is created and tried and, hopefully, those
served by the program will also be consulted and their input
included. This kind of process demonstrates the ends/means

confluence illustrated already, where individuals and communities are creators of their own change.

If, as a manager, you are worried that an individual (or more than one) on your team will be seen as better/smarter/more capable than you, or if you are overly concerned that those above you will not be open to the possibility of doing something differently to reach the mission, then you will probably quash ideas. Or if there is interest and you are worried about not looking good, you may imply to your higher-ups that new ideas were your ideas—even if they weren't. These are examples of actions that destroy trust and your credibility with your team and both are "managing up." In the first instance, protecting yourself by not making waves with new ideas and in the second, protecting yourself by stealing. Which, whether you realize it or not, your staff can see right through.

5.5.5 Transparency

Create a system to allow staff to see overall spending and income.

There are nonprofit organizations dedicated strictly to reviewing for-profit companies for fiscal transparency and good practices. Transparency International is one of the big ones, and they do an excellent job of uncovering corruption across sectors, including governments, industry, and civil society. Specifically within the nonprofit sector, GuideStar and Charity Navigator provide information on nonprofit finances and rate nonprofits based on fiscal soundness, accountability, transparency, and results. All information is readily available online, for free, and is oriented toward providing guidance to people who want to give to nonprofits. But what about providing information to team/staff members on the fiscal health of the organization?

If you were going to set up a system so that staff could see the organization's financials, what might your goals be?

Your concerns? Do you want staff to know how much *you* make? Too late if you are leading an organization and have a fully filled out 990 IRS form, it's listed online. What if you were directing more unrestricted funds toward one program than another, and you would have to justify this to those not getting more money? Controlling the finances of an organization can seat one in a position of complete power—fantastic, ultimate, untouchable, isolating power. It's why the world is in such a mess today, too few holding too much in secret off-shore accounts. No transparency.

Because we are not the for-profit sector, I would argue for as much fiscal transparency as possible within our organizations. As a nonprofit manager, this holds you accountable, and lets staff know where priorities or possible emerging areas of work lie. And those areas should be no surprise because if you are managing as mission, you have already discussed and decided on priorities and the implementation of those priorities with your team.

The one area that may not be an open (ledger) book is staff salaries, and you will need to ask your staff about this, given that research indicates both positive and negative ramifications of sharing salary information between staff. U.S. law states that staff cannot be terminated for asking about or discussing salaries with coworkers, and there is a strong legal leaning against a company's ability to create policies that prevent this discussion. If people are uncomfortable with disclosing individual amounts, salaries can be combined into a Personnel Service budget category, which shows the total salaries as part of the overall budget.

5.5.6 Equality and Justice

Apply all policies equally to all staff.

I've chosen to look at applying policies equally instead of some of the others ideas (equal pay for equal work) particularly because I'm just tired of talking and thinking about equal pay for equal work. Let's just say that in the world I want, people (and I mean ALL people) are represented in our organizations at all levels and that they are paid the same for the same job so that unity and not division is created (again, I have digressed from my one-idea rule; but being a woman, I had to make these points. What points? *Better representation and equal pay for equal work*). Thank you.

Let's look at applying policies equally to all staff. Are there set hours within which your team is supposed to work? Is there a flex-time policy? Can staff work from home? Do you have a team member who is producing great work but is late all the time? Or a person who is doing their job adequately and often has medical appointments with notes from the doctor? Or maybe someone who is not doing well and is asking for flex time that causes them to miss the weekly staff meeting? If you have managed staff, you have run into at least one of these dilemmas. They are in some ways very difficult and in others not so much, given that some policies are legally binding and others are at the discretion of the organization.

Let's focus on lateness. The first thing to do is to look at yourself to see if people are following your example, or the example of those above you. Do you come and go as you think the job warrants and not as policy requires? Are you late in the door in the morning or late to meetings? If so, you are going to have a difficult time asking your team to be on time. If this is not the case, and one person is coming in late on a regular basis, other team members see this and, even if that person is doing a great job, your team will at best wonder why you as manager are allowing this, and at worst become resentful and unmotivated and do less of a good job.

If someone is continually late, during our regular meeting I'd point out to them that they are doing a great job, and that I'm thinking something is going on because they have been late on a regular basis. I'd then ask if there is any way I can be helpful. Maybe school has started, and they have to drop off their son at the same time they are supposed to be at work. Perhaps they are caring for a sick parent, or are suffering from morning sickness and are tired of vomiting on the sidewalk on the way in. Or maybe they like to sleep in. Some jobs require people to be in a specific place at 8:30 or 9:00, and in others there may be some flexibility. As manager, it's your job to make sure the policies are followed by all, or there is flexibility for all, or to work to change policies if they are not appropriate. Working with your team members to figure out how to make it possible for them to do their work (unless they are sleeping in—then they need to buy an alarm clock ... or set their phone ... I'm so 1970s) can demonstrate equality and justice in the workplace.

5.5.7 Diversity

Hiring needs to reflect the mission.

Let's go back one last time to Oxfam's mission, *To create lasting solutions to poverty, hunger, and social injustice.* Who might need to be hired to reflect this mission?

In fact, you are going to need a whole host of people with different types of knowledge, skills, and experience to reach the mission and to be representative of that mission. If you've linked mission to process, you know a lot of the criteria for the people you will hire. Depending on the position, you will probably be looking for people who have values that reflect the organization's; have a long-term view of solving problems; are committed to the mission; and have experienced first-hand, or have worked directly with, people in situations of poverty, hunger, or injustice; ensuring there is a gender, ethnic and racial balance, avoiding child labor, and certifying that hiring is based on merit and not connection.

Hiring that reflects the mission may necessitate capacity development and making space for differing points of view, but if we are working to create the world we want, we are already with that program.

5.5.8 Freedom of Speech and Beliefs

5.5.8.1 Facilitation

Nonprofit people are often motivated by a passion to help, a passion for change. People working in advocacy and social justice organizations are by nature engaged in fighting systems and policies and often have no problem stating and advocating for their mission ... why, I have even done it myself on a number of occasions. I had my facts, my examples, and I told people about them and about what I had experienced on the ground. I had the technical knowledge and was happy to answer questions, and to push my point of view. That's why I was there, to make points that could ignite change! I was speaking truth to power! I was on a mission to tell them what they were doing wrong and how to do it the right way! I was on a mission—and maybe if I had thought about it a bit more, I could have made the same points with a little less blame thrown in. Of course, there is a time and a place for this kind of intervention; however, if within our organizations we are approaching one another with the same mindset as we approach advocacy targets, team members may find themselves shut down by other team members who are louder or more experienced, or just need to be *right*.

As manager, it will be your job to facilitate meetings and, hopefully, to model skills that provide a safe space for people to express ideas. You might also create a policy that provides the opportunity for everyone on the team to facilitate meetings on a rotating basis. This builds skills, shares power and control, and makes people aware of behaviors in the team that help or hold back progress in meetings.

In my experience in nonprofits, facilitation is a highly underrated skill—kind of like managing—it is often not taught in education programs and, unless one has been in a situation where it has been demonstrated (or you have a natural ability), how could you know how to do it? How to create an agenda that leads to outcomes? How to let people share ideas for ways forward *and* keep the meeting on schedule, to moderate differences in opinion *and* maintain working relationships.

Hopefully, the facilitator is prepared because they have seen good facilitation from others in the team or on staff. They are able to suspend (but are not disregarding) their own ideas about the ways forward so that they can listen to others, synthesize what they are hearing, keep the discussion on track, and ensure everyone has the opportunity for input.

If one of your staff is regularly "talked over" by others, you might want to have a chat with that person to find out about their experience in meetings. Or it may be obvious that one person is dominating the dialogue. If that is the case, one person dominating, it's your job to talk to them, one-on-one, to give some positive feedback about their enthusiasm, and then to ask if they are aware of how much they speak and what their impact might be on the process of discussion and decision-making. There are courses on facilitation and books on the dynamics of groups; take a look online or ask a colleague for recommendations.

5.5.9 Sustainable Production and Consumption

Ensure staff are working reasonable hours and are taking vacations.

In the for-profit sector, as I was shocked to learn from my husband, people get two weeks off annually when they start a new job. Part of the reason for my surprise was that my dad, who as I said before worked for Budweiser while I was growing up, got multiple weeks off each year. I can't remember if it was five or six, but it was enough so that we could go on vacation and he could paint houses on the side for extra income. Why did he have so much vacation? It was because of the union. As a manager, it may seem heretical for me to support unions; however, it's not so much that I support unions as I support what they stand for: some equity in the power relationship between the owners and the workers (am I sounding like Marx?—no, Marx wanted workers to own the means of production—I'm just looking for equity). Living wages. Good working conditions. Realistic working hours. Time off. Compensation for on-the-job injuries. Some matching funds for retirement, given most of us no longer have pensions associated with our jobs. Benefits, although I would very much like benefits to be de-linked from employment and provided by the government. Ok, I'm sounding more like a "socialist" now. A democratic socialist. I always say that if I am very, very, VERY good in this life, in my next life I will come back as a Norwegian. Where there is democratic socialism. And fjords.

Staff need vacation to recharge. Work in the nonprofit sector is often service delivery: support for children that have been abused; providing food to people living on the street; cleaning up after oil spills; advocating for returning veterans. Service delivery is hard work, cognitively, emotionally, and sometimes physically. If people are not rested, given the opportunity to unwind, they are not going to be doing the best job they can. At some point, they will burn out and you will lose them: they will quit or you will have to let them go.

Ensuring that your team takes their vacation is critically important for ensuring the mission is met, and it is also a signal to your staff that you respect that they have lives outside of work, that they are human and need rest. It sets a tone of balance, and these are messages you want your staff to send to those with whom they work.

How do you do this when a dilemma with nonprofit staff is that they are mission-driven and often cannot "shut down" enough to take holidays? Truly, we are often our own worst enemies. Nonprofit workers ask, *"How can we be ok taking a vacation when the horrors of the world continue?"* This is a valid point. People running from war don't get time off. Nor do women who have been raped or veterans who have lost limbs. Individuals working for a cause have to come to terms with this in their own ways, and as a manager, you need to grapple with this yourself, and then help your team with their struggles. One-to-one discussions, team discussions, organization-wide discussions can help. So can having clear policies about vacations, holidays, sick time, personal days, and so on.

Establish a process for keeping track of days taken by your team to make sure people are taking vacations. Post a calendar of organization-wide holidays somewhere that everyone can see. This is easier when all staff are in one country, because holidays will be consistent. If staff are in different countries, you will have to work out separate holiday schedules with different staff members. If you are in a large organization, Human Resources will have figured this out or will help you figure it out. If not, you need to make sure that there is enough parity between staff so that everyone is being treated fairly. I ran a network where people were hired by different agencies; some people received five weeks' vacation, and others three. Although there was not a lot I could do about it given each person was under the human resources policies of that organization, we arranged at-home "reading/ writing days" so the staff that weren't getting the longer holidays had the opportunity to be away from email and phones, and to delve into a job-related area of their interest. This was not ideal, but helped a little to balance the disparity.

When a vacation is in the future of one of your team members, plan with them prior to their leaving. What needs to be done while they are off? Are there any crises that might be avoided by having someone check in on a person/situation? Is there a deadline that needs to be met? There are options for each of these. If a caseload is involved, make sure that someone (or someones) is covering the caseload. If the person is in development (fundraising), make sure all deadline dates are known, and assign responsibilities to others as they are able. Or, do it yourself.

It's always a good idea to have contact information for your staff when they are away; however, I tell people that unless there is a major crisis—the building burning down (which may not mandate a call since they can't do anything about this anyway) or a death—I will not call or be in touch with them while they are away. I ask that they put an "out of office" message on their phone and email, and refer anyone to me (or the covering person) if help is needed. This way, covering staff are clear about their responsibilities, and the person going on vacation can truly relax knowing the work will be done.

Leading by example is another key. Take your time off. Plan well before you leave so that your team will be as up-to-date as possible and will be able to fill in during your vacation. Even with this, you will probably need to be available by phone or email unless you have an associate/deputy or someone to whom you report; if you do, hopefully they will have the same orientation to time off as you and will work to pick up your responsibilities when you are away. If not, being available comes with the territory of management. Sorry, that's why they pay you the big bucks (LOL).

Oh, and in the interest of sustainable production and consumption, get some recycle bins if you don't have them.

5.6 Managing As Mission, Differing Expectations, and Dealing with the Tough Stuff

In all jobs, as in life, people have expectations. Some expectations are based in reality, some are not. As a younger person fresh out of graduate school, I wanted to run an international organization. Never mind that I had very little experience working in an organization and almost no international work experience; I had a Master's degree and had interned at the UN, and that seemed like enough. I had no idea what I did not know. And based on that knowledge deficit, I believed that I could do a job that now, with 25 years of hindsight and experience in my pocket, I realize would have been a disaster for me, for anyone I was managing, and for the people being served by the organization. I had big expectations that did not match my level of experience or knowledge.

A good manager knows how to, well, *manage* team/staff expectations while at the same time encouraging them to move ahead to realize their individual goals as well as the organizational mission. To recognize and acknowledge that people are not just in this for the paycheck, and to help guide them through the working relationship, to where they want to go in their lives and careers (treating people as they want to be treated). This is mentoring. Coaching. Not everyone wants this; some of your staff may just want to do their jobs and are less interested in careers or moving ahead. The only way to know how interested people are is to observe and to ask.

We've looked at the manager's role in managing as mission and all the good that can come from it, but we haven't talked a whole lot about what happens when there are problems at work. On your team. In your office. Unhappy staff. Role dissatisfaction. Non-team-oriented individuals.

Ugh.

There have been times when I've been overtired and frustrated, and have thought to myself, "I don't care if X is happy, they're being paid to do a job and they need to get busy. They need to get with the program!" Yes, I have thought this. Just as I have thought "If my daughter does not clean her room/wash those dishes/come home on time/add your own, I'm going to strangle her!" Do I really mean it? No. It's an indication that I'm hugely frustrated and, probably, that I've either not been paying attention to what's happening or I have tried a number of interventions with limited success.

Is it important for staff to be happy? Overall, yes. As shown previously by research, happy staff perform better. And they are, well, HAPPY. And nice to be around. Maybe they make jokes and everyone laughs. They are not trash talking or giving you—or anyone else—the stink-eye. The work environment can make a job more appealing, and can contribute to increased morale leading to even better work. In a recent study of workers in the UK, "pay" came in below "good relationship with colleagues," "enjoying the job role," "good relationship with my boss," "I don't have another job to go to," and "my commute is manageable" (Boren, 2014). If you want the mission to be met, having people who are happy/satisfied with their jobs is part of meeting the mission. No one is happy all the time, but the work environment is a much better place in which to function when people are mostly happy.

From my experience and from interviews, conversation, and the academic literature, if staff are unhappy, it's most likely for one of three reasons:

1. There is a problem with the organizational system.
2. There is a problem with the manager.
3. The job is not a good fit for the person.

1. *Problem with Organizational System*

This is going to be short because we've talked about a lot of this previously. If there are problems with the organization's systems, you may be able to work to change them, you may be able to create an oasis for your team by "running interference" between them and the hierarchy, you may give up and become part of the dysfunction, or you might quit. You know what you can tolerate and what you can't, and if you've tried to make changes and have been unsuccessful, you know your options.

2. *Problems with the Manager*

Micromanager. Blamer. Bully. Isolator. Gossiper. As a manager, you've most likely had other managers. What have they done that has made you better able to do your job? What have they done that has hindered your ability to get the work done? Thinking about this, even writing down what was helpful and not helpful, can be a starting point for you as a manager. The caveat here is that what worked for you might not work for someone else; you might have really appreciated a manager that checked in with you every day, multiple times a day.

Someone else may not like, or need, that kind of oversight, especially if they have experience in their job. But write it down anyway, it's a good place to start.

Are you having the same problems with your team in your current organization that you've had before? Does your team avoid making eye contact (not a problem in some cultures)? Are their answers short? Do they avoid meetings? If this is the case, I'd ask myself about my role and actions in the work relationship. Is there something I am doing that is creating a lack of trust? Am I stifling participation by solely pushing my ideas? Am I trying to make change faster than people are prepared to move? Do I listen? Do I ask questions, or do I tell people what to do? Am I at all interested in my team as individuals? In their future? Does my team feel safe enough to disagree? If you see consistency in patterns, the difficulty might be your modus operandi, which you can change.

Managing involves letting staff know how they are doing on a regular basis. This is where managers/supervisors often find their greatest challenges. Are you very good at praising but not so good at talking with a team member on how they could do something better or think about something in a different way? Is it easier for you to be critical, pointing out deficits, and thinking that people know what they've done well? Are you somewhere in between? Although there are a whole bunch of problematic issues that a manager can bring to a team or a workplace, we'll talk about micromanaging, elitism, and denying there are problems.

As a manager, one of your primary jobs is to make sure all work is leading to and reflective of the mission. It's your job to strike a balance between support, monitoring, encouraging, setting good boundaries, and, sometimes, giving difficult feedback. Staff need enough oversight to get their jobs done but not so much that they feel micromanaged—because this will lead to feeling frustrated and incompetent, and unless someone is not doing their job, micromanaging is never about the team member, it's about the manager needing to be in control in exceedingly unhelpful ways. Are you driven to check on what people are doing multiple times a day? Are you always telling them how to do things "differently/better"? Do people need to run their emails by you before you hit send? Then unless you are … no, wait … I was going to write "a brain surgeon" or "the National Security Agency," but even there, unless you have a team member that is just starting out, if you are doing these things, you need to let go. Stop. Pull it back. People become resentful, quickly disempowered, and then they work to get their needs filled in different ways. They resign themselves to the situation which makes for a complete lack of creative thought and a subculture of frustration resulting in anger, and/or they quit; neither are good outcomes and are completely counter to the ethical treatment of humans, animals, and the planet.

Are you "above" certain tasks in your organization? Your team needs to know that you would not ask them to do anything you would not do yourself. Is the toilet clogged? Would you pick up the plunger or will you ask someone else to do it (unless it is specifically within another person's job description or it is skill-specific; I'd never try to fix wiring)? How about making coffee for a meeting? Again, if this is in your admin/ support person's job description that may be ok, but doing this yourself, or for example offering to support one of your team by running to get copies while they are facilitating a meeting, says that as manager, we respect the work they are doing and we want them to be successful.

Is everything perfect in your organization? Idealizing your situation can be as bad as if you are constantly complaining. Why? Because no situation is perfect (remember Affiliative managing style …). There are almost always problems. They are not necessarily problems of internal politics, who's doing a good job, who's not, who is the favorite of a manager (which is a huge problem) and who is not, who gets away with things and who does not; problems also come from the external environment: lack of funding, competition from other organizations with a similar mandate in the same location (yes, there is competition between not-for-profits, just like between for-profits—we have to show we are doing a good job so that we will continue to be funded: no money, no mission).

If you are denying problems within your job/organization, you will make your team crazy. They know there are problems. There are *always* problems; that's why nonprofits exist, to address problems. Staff have problems in getting their jobs done due to things outside of their control. They have problems with one another. They have problems in their work with those served by the organization. Budget problems, power and control problems; and they have life problems that, try as they might not to, they may bring to work. As their manager, they bring them to you. You deny there are problems. They feel crazy. Frustrated. Angry. If you are not acknowledging these issues, and you are hoping that everything is going to work itself out without your intervention, the subsequent failures that will occur rest squarely on your lack-of-management shoulders. This is not managing as mission.

3. *Job is Not a Good Fit*

We often think of a team member as being "difficult" or "problematic" because it's easier for us to blame the person than to work to fix the system (if possible) or to look at the impact our thoughts or behaviors are having on others, or to help the person find a job that's a better fit whether inside or outside the organization. Each of these requires additional work and, in nonprofit organizations, people are often strapped for time and resources.

There are times when a staff person is just not a good fit for their current position. I'm not describing incidents that are violations of law or ethics; these infractions need to be dealt with swiftly. I'm referring to a person who might have been doing a good job and there has been a change, or someone who has been hired and is not up to the job. Maybe they are bored, they don't have enough responsibility. Perhaps they are in over their head. Maybe they are unmotivated toward work in general. Or maybe there is inequity in salaries; as Rosabeth Moss Kanter (2013), a Harvard Business School professor and author writing in the *Harvard Business Review*, states,

> Money can even be an irritant if compensation is not adequate or fair, and compensation runs out of steam quickly as a source of sustained performance.

You can take the approach that it is not your job to determine why someone is performing poorly; your way of managing might include the idea that your team members need to *do their job* or leave/be terminated. In the private sector if you are not producing, if your sales levels dive, or if you keep knocking cans of Coke off of the assembly line and holding up progress, you might find yourself out of a job (maybe I'm being too harsh on the private sector … nah …). But a sudden termination, "firing" in the old days, without a process leading up to it can be a soul-shattering experience, never mind the financial burden it places on an individual/family.

If someone is not doing their job well, I want to know why. Do they need additional training, knowledge, or skills? Do they understand their job description and the responsibilities associated with it? Do they understand how the organization works? Are they being bullied by someone on staff? Are they in the throes of a divorce, or has there been a recent death in their close circle? Are they caring for a sick relative? If any of these, or something similar, is the case for poor performance, I want to talk with the person to determine if there is something we as the organization can do to help. Family Medical Leave Act? Flex hours? Capacity development courses? Move to part time if the workload allows, or create a shared position?

If there is nothing of significance happening, or if your team member is not willing to cite causes or take advantage of suggestions, it's time to start documenting the poor performance. Which is miserable. It takes a lot of time and attention to specific acts (or non-acts), because anything you talk about with your team member should be grounded in examples. And you actually have to have difficult con-versations with the person about the examples you have observed.

None of this should come as a surprise to either you or your team member. Your regular meetings will have included reviews of what has been done and what needs to be done, and, if you have asked and things are not getting done and the person can't explain the reasons, the next steps should be no surprise. Review their job description with them. Ask if there are areas where they see themselves as doing well and others where they may need help. Set targets for the next week, and in your next meeting review the targets. Were they met? And if you have a human resource department, please check with them before you take any action at all.

Once you have talked to them to determine if there are ways they can be successful, have pulled out the job descrip-tion, and are documenting their work (or lack thereof), your team member knows that

- You are serious about meeting the mission.
- You want them to succeed.
- You are consistent and will follow through.
- They will need to get to work.
- Or, they will need to look for another job or be let go.

Most of the time, by the time you've reviewed the job description and documented performance, people will have started to look for another job. None of this has to be mean or harsh on your part and, in fact, it shouldn't be. This is about managing as mission—helping someone move to another position where they will be able to do a better job (hopefully), and your team will be able to meet the organiza-tional mission.

5.7 Summary

Laying it out, managing as mission is

- An organizationally defined picture of the world the organization wants
- Those inside and served by the organization being clear about that big picture—because they have helped create it
- Deciding on and acting in accordance with the values, ethics, and process statement created by those in and served by the organization
- Thinking and acting as though the process and the mission are one
- As a manager, working with my team and others in ways that uphold and reflect these ideas

You've done a lot of work while reading this chapter. You have envisioned what the world might look like if specific management styles prevailed. You have considered the limitations of "mission" as it relates to process, and have learned how to go beyond mission, linking it to the world one wants. Then you worked backward from there, thinking about language and how language impacts ways of working and managing. After giving language to the world you want, you then went on to delineate managing behaviors that might get you, your team, your organization, and those served by the organization, to that world. You considered how to embody and implement managing as mission from the first meeting and through times when difficulties arise.

By doing these exercises, you've engaged in a process—the same kind of process described in Chapter III—and if you have done it seriously, there will be at least a few things you will do differently in your managing role. Even a few changes can make a difference, so look for changes in your team and be kind to yourself and acknowledge yourself (in your mind and heart) when you've actually done something differently. As a reward, maybe a Krispy Kreme vanilla crème donut?

Maybe just "well done you!" in the interest of good health.

Chapter VI

What Can Come from Managing As Mission

Managing as mission. Might it be possible to change the world, at least your part of it, through managing? Through what is seen as boring bureaucracy? Removed from the *real* work? Within the existing structure?

Yes.

If you are clear and motivated regarding your managing role being reflective of a better world, you will act differently than you have in the past. And your impact on others will be different and, hopefully, their impact on others will be different, because everyone has had a say in the mission, processes, work, and managing. If this is clear, you will have an easier time managing and will be able to focus on other things like, say, raising money or planning evaluations or looking at new articles on how to do the work even better. And because your team is clear and united, they will listen to you, to one another, and, most importantly, to those served by the organization.

Managing as mission is all about you, and it's not about you at all. It's change and consistency. It's mission as means and ends. It's holding what you know and being willing to accept what others know. It's a paradox wrapped in an enigma inside a conundrum housed in … oh I don't know … it's somewhere in the middle and all around the outside. It's being able to hold multiple ideas and truths, including yours, and give them similar weight and respect in work and decision-making. It's about creating a small "world we want" right here, right now.

So specifically, what can come from managing as mission?

Moving away from an outdated, outmoded mission-as-ends paradigm.

Inherent in managing as mission is the movement away from the idea of mission as rooted in a top-down, authoritarian, special/ separate, potentially ego-driven, and static system (closed, we bring the answers, we have the right way of doing things), toward a transparent, inclusive way of working—collaboration—that provides greater equality and less separation. Everyone, including those served by the organization and staff, bring their piece of the truth and are part of creating the process of how the organization does its work. Everyone is clear about where the organization is going and how it's getting there. That clarity provides the ongoing opportunity to refine the mission to reflect the ever-changing circumstance of those served and the ever-growing knowledge base concerning what works. It can stop mission creep before it starts and/or allow for new ideas for growth.

The shift in thinking about mission, in and of itself, has the potential to transform the direction and substance of communication and contribute to different behaviors, and mandates a different way of working that opens the door for diverse ideas on problem-solving, establishing goals, and the methods for reaching them.

A demonstration that the world we want is possible.

Okay so you've got people and you've got money and you have to bring those two things together in a meaningful way that creates a positive outcome for a person, place or thing maybe all three. Then you get [to the idea of] a positive outcome. In my frame of reference, a positive outcome is something that nourishes both the micro and macro levels of life, something that makes an individual better and something that makes a system better. We're back to common good, or back to the relationship between what individuals do and the common good ... [And as a manager] how do I make that happen? I want something that creates and enriches both an individual's life, and our collective lives. (Interviewee)

Managing as mission can allow the people on your team to experience a better world, one where the worth, dignity, and equality of each person are lifted up through an I-Thou relationship. If people experience this happening in one place, they know that at least some form of it can happen elsewhere.

Credibility within and outside the organization.
As one interviewee said,

I can't go into a room to talk with a partner to talk about how we need to find their agency and voice within the work if I go back to my office and I'm like "Hey, you need to do that, you need to get me that now." You can't do that because the partner is going to [see] that [in] your email trails and everything like that, people are going to find out. "You're not living up to that, not doing that, why should I as a partner trust you to follow through on the work?" So it goes to a very practical application to manage consistently to the mission.

If we have created a world we want inside the organization, people outside will see this and will know that this is a group that walks the walk. Because of a consultative process regarding values, ethics, ideas, and processes, people will feel ownership and will want to ensure that the way work is done is as important as reaching the goal. Negative chatter will be minimized. People from other organizations will see this, and will want to work for your organization.

Respectful relationships founded on trust both within the organization and from staff to those served.
Managing as mission is founded on the creation of a matrix of relationships that are grounded in trust, and trust is built on consistency, clarity, openness, and integrity. As a manager, if you are consistent in your behaviors, clear in your communications and the ways in which you work, open to others' ideas, and uphold the team-created values and ethics statements as well as the mission, those around you *will* notice. And they will have a much better chance to incorporate and embrace those characteristics within themselves. Another interviewee said,

> and so really creating a sense for leadership to create a sense of buy-in and trust and autonomy within a staff so that the work can carry on as it's meant to, with staff feeling supported and included in every decision-making facet.

Oh, and if your team trusts one another, they're probably going to be happier, and we know that happy staff create better results than unhappy staff.

Understanding of what those served are being asked to do: change.
Managing as mission is based on the idea of change, individual, group, and organizational. Not change for the sake of change, but change as an outcome of relating process and managing to mission. Creating a Values Statement and Code of Ethics is a step toward change. Engaging in "I-Thou" instead of "I-It" includes a willingness to suspend one's own beliefs to arrive at something new. Listening makes change possible. The deep empathy and humility gained from the experience of what it means to change motivates people to show kindness when they see others working to change. This is not "cutting people slack," it is understanding that change is difficult, lifting up successes, and allowing room for "misses" with a

process in place for assessing how success might be reached the next time.

One of my favorite statements from the interviews was about change:

> But here's the kicker they [managers] are so miserable
> most of the time, with the reality of their jobs, that
> why the hell wouldn't they want to look for a new
> solution? Why the hell wouldn't they want to look for
> another style of management that would work better?
> Why the hell wouldn't they think about ways to make
> it better? And I agree with you this translates into
> change. When you are as unhappy as I think many,
> many people are out there, with what's going on in
> their work lives, I don't then know how you can make
> it better if you can't consider other ways to do things.

Reduction in the fear/hope dichotomy through transparency and trust.

Managing as mission provides an opportunity to move beyond the fear/hope dichotomy through trust and transparency. If you know the rules, if they apply to everyone and they have been created collaboratively based on the mission, values, ethics, and law, if you have a clear job description, if you know the fiscal health of the organization, then you know where you are and what is possible within the organization. You are aware of possible career trajectories (or lack of) and whether the organization is healthy enough that you don't have to look for another job.

And although fear/hope will never be eliminated—nor should they be—reducing the dichotomy, especially in people like me who are anxious and worry all the time, can make for a more organized and coherent stream of work. If I'm always scanning the environment, if I don't know what the possibilities are, if my job description overlaps with other people, work is not going to be accomplished efficiently and effectively.

As a bit of an aside, I wonder if I would have pushed myself as hard as I have if I didn't have that anxious, nagging little (ok BIG) voice inside that, to this day, keeps asking, "But what if ..." or "Maybe this would be better ..." or "let me try that a different way." And if I had no hope that things could get better, I probably would not say those same things to myself because I wouldn't care. So hope and fear (but especially hope) *are* important drivers, but they need to be greatly tempered and not used as mechanisms to hold down or control yourself, your team, or those served by the organization.

Role models for managers-to-be.
One interviewee said,

> And I think a lot of times people have no role models. There's nobody that they've ever experienced or that is doing it in a way that is actually uplifting. And that's a big part of it. So if you have never experienced it, how do you know what to do?

Whether you manage as mission or not, you will be a role model for your team and others who see how and what you are doing. People learn by their exposure to others and "what you show, you sow" (hey! I just made that up—I think). As part of process, you'll ask your team what would be helpful for them regarding managing, both in the relationship with you as their manager as well as what they want to learn about being a manager (if they do plan to manage someday).

Setting aside some time in your regular meetings to talk about managing, collecting information that can be disseminated, having a managing seminar so that staff can gather ideas and have role-playing experience can be really helpful. If you or your organization do any of these, you've got role modeling taking place; it demonstrates your commitment to the growth of staff and a commitment to constructive change.

6.1 Finale

Here we are at the end, and there is so much we haven't covered! Strategic planning, dashboards, business plans, team retreats, measurement, conflict, performance reviews, annual increases, innovative fundraising, micromanaging, meetings, so many things. But as I wrote before, you are busy, and this book is long enough.

Just a couple of last words.

When I started this book, I was not thinking about the idea of managing as mission as a transformative process ... *transformative* ... another buzzword that I thought was in the dictionary next to "new age" and "crystal healing." Then, one of the people interviewed said,

> I think that we have focused so much on structure, organizational structure, and restructuring ... and I think that leadership and management are integrally connected on all levels, no matter where you are as a manager, you are a leader. Or you're part of a team. It's really so much about how you approach things, and ... I'm going to say if what is happening at the top, whatever the structure is, is not open and inclusive, not reflective of the mission, then it's going to be very hard for people to actually make that kind of personal transformation so that the big transformation can happen.

And as I talked to more people, and read, and thought, it slowly dawned on me that managing *can* be about transformation: changing the thoughts, values, beliefs, and behaviors that emerge from a deliberate way of interacting with others. That change is contagious. As someone who has changed in many ways through being managed by people who were deeply committed to their roles and the betterment of program through the growth of staff, as well as having managed staff from whom I learned so much, I have striven to manage others in ways that I hope have lifted them, supported and encouraged their ideas and work, and, ultimately, improved program outcomes and set an example for the next generation of managers.

If as a manager, you take this on, if you work to manage as mission, you will step into a place of some struggle, some frustration; you will make mistakes, and you will lose some sleep. Be as kind as possible to yourself and to your team. Apologize when you are wrong—this is not a sign of weakness unless you are using apologizing as a way of not changing; a genuine apology can actually be a display of great strength.

From the struggle, you will understand what it means to change, and you will model this for others. You will understand for yourself what you are asking others to do. And it can feel absolutely wonderful—I think this is what children experience when they are playing and building on an invented game (somehow we always think of change through listening to others or coming from cooperation as diminishing—it's not MY IDEA, I can't take full credit, someone may know better than me …). If you feel diminished, please ask yourself why—there's a lot to be learned for all of us.

If you manage as mission, you will internalize what it means to lift others up by giving credit where credit is due, providing positive and constructive feedback.

You will learn a lot about how other people think, and you will see that there are many interesting, creative, successful ways to get to a goal.

You will be trusted by people who otherwise might see your role as authoritarian, as having power over them, and you will learn to trust them.

You will create a world within your organization that is the world in which you—and your team through their participation in creating it—want to live.

So you see, there's actually a lot in it for you if you manage as mission.

You can do it. I'm rooting for you.

Chapter VII

Tools

This chapter section brings together tools in the book. They are

- Exercise 1: Working Relationships
- Exercise 2: What Would the World Look Like if It Were Managed Like ...
- Exercise 3: Managing, Mission, and Process: Getting to the World We Want
- Exercise 4: Work Behaviors That Reflect the World the Organization Wants
- Exercise 5: Generating Possible Managing Behaviors Based on the World We Want

7.1 Exercise 1: Working Relationships

Relationships at work need to function in ways that mirror the mission/world we want. Listed next are a few examples of relationships; in the blanks following, add the people and things (processes, systems, etc.) that you might imagine having to manage, or are currently managing. Please do not feel constrained by the spaces provided, write in as many or as few as you can think of.

- Person to themselves (including you)
- Staff to you as manager
- Staff to staff
- Staff to those served
- Those served to staff
- Staff to the work
- You to fundraising
- Finance to you
- Finance to staff
- Staff to mission and vision
- You to technology
- You to external systems
- _____
- _____
- _____
- _____
- _____
- _____
- _____
- _____
- _____
- _____
- _____

Now that you have a list, determine if there *is or is not* interaction and whether there *needs* to be interaction. Write your mission at the top of the page, choose one interaction, then ask yourself the questions

- How do these interactions take place now?
- How might these interactions be viewed as "I-Thou" relationships?

■ How would viewing them as relationships, as a reflection of the mission, change the way interactions take place?

7.2 Exercise 2: What Would the World Look Like if It Were Managed Like …

Different managing styles may be needed for different work-places, tasks, individuals. And although no manager reflects solely one style, an individual's personality does impact how they manage, tilting them more toward one style than another.

Described next are three different managing styles: Directive, Affiliative, and Managing by Walking Around. Either individually or in teams, read the description of each style and write down what the world would look like if it were managed in that style.

7.2.1 Directive Managing

A Directive manager is described as a person who is clear about what they see needing to be done, defines expectations, sets rules, and gives directions. In a less favorable light, directive managing can manifest as coercive, controlling, demanding compliance, and a 'do as I tell you' methodology enforced by threats.

A directively managed world would probably look a lot like basic training in the army. There would be a centralized authority that made the rules and dictated what needed to be done and how to do it. From growing crops to creating microchips, things would be done in a specific way, leading to a lot of rules and regulations for everything in life. Maybe down to brushing your teeth. Which would have the potential of restricting creative or inventive thought, and there would be people who would not fit in and would want to rebel—but as in basic training, you would conform or you would go AWOL and be court-martialed and jailed. Or if you learned great survival skills, you might make it in the desert or the woods, but what fun would that be long term? Unless there were others like you, and now we have a dystopian young adult novel so let's leave it there.

You most likely would not have a lot of close relationships with those outside your group, whether you were the director or the directee, and would probably better relate to people who are "on your level" or doing what you do—either because there is not a lot of room for movement up, or because you have been indoctrinated to maintain your place in the world. Or both. You might have a great deal of trust in those providing direction if you are more comfortable as a worker than a manager—which is completely acceptable and much needed in the world—if the person providing direction is transparent and provides what you need to get the job done. And a lot of work would get done because expectations and methodologies would be clear and stated, and you would do the work because someone had directed you to do it. Or you might live in a state of fear, of being threatened by others if you don't stick with the program. And even if you have good ideas, they may never be heard because "it's not the way we do things here."

7.2.2 Affiliative Managing

An affiliative manager is one who is great at team-building, creating trust, connecting people, raising morale, providing positive and minimizing negative feedback, and is less likely to want to deal with problems and conflict. What might a world look like if it ran on an affiliative model?

Affiliative managing sounds great initially. People would be lifted up, happiness and getting along would be the goal, people would feel linked to one another and, hopefully, to the environment. Doors to houses would remain unlocked because people would trust one another. In the affiliative world, people would be loyal to the person in charge because everyone would get an award, and who doesn't want an award? Even if you are not doing a great job, you are still part of the team and can get the same award as everyone else. And if everyone is the same, if all get awards, there shouldn't be conflict, right?

Maybe after multiple millennia, if we haven't completely mucked up the planet and destroyed ourselves, we might not engage in the kinds of behaviors, internal or external, that lead to conflict. The dilemma is that as of now we are all human and, although we are made from the same stuff as the Dalai Lama, most of us (myself included in a big way) are operating within a values system that may not be absolutely clear to us, or may require us to change our values and subsequent behaviors. If we have not learned how to successfully navigate conflict, and if there is a rub, a twinge of internal discomfort leading to an inner dilemma, we may not be prepared to deal with the situation, denying or repressing the conflicting feeling. Which can lead to inertia: a world where things don't change because people cannot deal with differences of opinion. A world of frustration because problems don't get solved.

7.2.3 Managing by Walking Around

Management by Walking Around was a fundamental modality at Hewlett-Packard, where both Hewlett and Packard randomly and in an unstructured way walked around the company asking questions and getting ideas. What would a world look like where, instead of people in their office sending emails to people 10 feet from them, they got up and walked around and talked to everyone at least part of the time, asked questions, listened, and then as much as possible, attempted to respond to needs and take on ideas?

As social beings, humans form relationships. Studies show that if there are positive relationships with coworkers and supervisors, job performance increases. A world reflective of managing by walking around implies that there is an accepted structure, and that in contrast to telling people what to do and how to do it, there is a genuine interest on the part of those who are in charge to know about how things are working in the day-to-day of doing one's job and what people think about the best ways forward. It implies less of a gap between those in charge and everyone else. In a world created by "walking around," political leaders would regularly hold town hall meetings, attend events like pancake breakfasts, go to workplaces, and actually listen to their constituents. It is not unlike United States democracy, where politicians attend meetings to "take the pulse" of their home districts. It is different in that in the world, leaders in democracies are elected, and in corporations, the founder/owner/CEO is not (in most cases) elected and gets a larger share of the wealth than those being asked for their opinions. (Maybe not so different from democratic politics …) And it works when what people say is acted upon by those asking the questions. People would probably feel valued, they would think critically, barriers would be lessened between people. I'm sure there are downsides in this world, the implication is that control and compensation remain the same, but it seems there would be a better chance of cracking that hierarchy if people felt valued, could see change being made based on their ideas, and then felt empowered to do more.

7.3 Exercise 3: Managing, Mission, and Process: Getting to the World We Want

Getting to the world you want to see can take the form of a discussion that includes those served by the organization, the staff, and hopefully the board. It's big picture, visionary. This discussion has the potential to be both expansive and digressive, and your job as manager—especially if you are facilitating—is to ensure that it comes back to the mission of the organization and what *that* means for the world you want to see.

You'll need a facilitator and a note-taker, and the exercise will take from one to two hours.

Getting to the world the organization wants begins with a set of big-picture questions that can then be defined. You might want to brainstorm questions prior to doing the exercise. Some of those questions might be

■ What would a person's life look like in the world we want?
■ What does the planet look like in the world we want?
■ What would relationships look like in the world we want?

You might want to think economically, socially, healthcare-wise, educationally, in terms of information, housing, nourishment, water, environment, and so on. You can create a statement from the results of the conversation, or you can leave the answers in categorized lists based on your questions. Putting the world your organization wants into categories will provide easier access to that information for later exercises.

7.4 Exercise 4: Work Behaviors That Reflect the World the Organization Wants

This exercise uses your work on beliefs, values, mission, process, and the world the organization wants, to consider behaviors toward those served by the organization.

Insert the world your organization wants in the first column, the beliefs and values you have delineated in your Values Statement, and your mission in the mission column. Then, based on the world you want and your beliefs and values, brainstorm a view of those the organization serves. When the group has finished this, move on to brainstorm behaviors that would best reflect the view of those served through the lens of the organizational mission.

The World We Want	Beliefs	Values	View of Those Served	Organizational Mission	Behaviors toward Those Served

7.5 Exercise 5: Generating Possible Managing Behaviors Based on the World We Want

This exercise is designed to help new as well as experienced managers take the ideas within the world we want and go beyond managing orientation to get to specific behaviors reflective of those ideas. Start with an idea from your list of the world one wants, then consider how that impacts your ideas about your staff/team/other relationships, think about the questions raised and then possible behavioral responses related to the idea/team/questions:

The World We Want	Beliefs/ Values	My View of Those on My Team/in My Organization	Mission	Questions to Ask as a Manager	Possible Managing Behaviors

Bibliography

Abrashoff, Michael D. 2002. *It's Your Ship: Management Techniques from the Best Damn Ship in the Navy.* New York: Warner Books.

ACER (Australian Council for Educational Research). 2015. Citizen-Led Educational Monitoring Shows Promise. Article, *International Developments*, 6, no. 8 (July). http://research.acer.edu.au/intdev/vol6/iss6/8.

Acumen. 2016. Mission Statement. http://acumen.org/.

Adams, Douglas. 1982. *Life, The Universe and Everything.* New York: Harmony Books.

Alkahtani, Ali Hussein; Abu-Jarad, Ismael; Sulaiman, Mohamed; and Nikbin, Davoud. 2011. Personality and Leadership Styles on Leading Change Capability of Malaysian Managers. Article, *Australian Journal of Business and Management Research*, 1, no. 2 (May). http://www.ajbmr.com/articlepdf/ajbmr_v01n02_06.pdf.

Allen, T. F. H. 2001. Hierarchy theory in Ecology. *Encyclopedia of Environmetrics.* Wiley. NJ: Wiley.

Amjad, Zahra; Sabri, Pirzada Sami Ullah; Ilyas, Muhammad; and Hameed, Afshaan. 2015. Informal Relationships at Workplace and Employee Performance: A Study of Employees Private Higher Education Sector. Article, *Pakistan Journal of Commerce and Social Sciences*, 9, no. 1: 303–321.

Anderson, Cameron and Brown, Courtney E. 2010. The Functions and Dysfunctions of Hierarchy. Article, *Research in Organizational Behavior.* University of California at Berkeley. http://haas.berkeley.edu/faculty/papers/anderson/functions%20and%20dysfunctions%20of%20hierarchy.pdf.

Anderson, Howard. 2004. Why Big Companies Can't Invent. Article, *MIT Technology Review*. https://www.technologyreview. com/s/402693/why-big-companies-cant-invent/.

Blood:Water. 2014. Mission Statement. http://www.bloodwater.org/.

Boren, Zachary Davies. 2014. British Workers Want Friends Not Money, According to New Study. Article, The *Independent*. http://www.independent.co.uk/life-style/health-and-families/ health-news/british-workers-want-friends-not-money-according- to-new-study-9940531.html.

Buber, Martin. 2000. *I and Thou*. New York: Scribner Classics.

Business Dictionary. 2016. Definition of Management. Entry. http:// www.businessdictionary.com/definition/management.html.

Cambridge Dictionary. 2016. Definition of Mission. Entry. http://dic- tionary.cambridge.org/us/dictionary/english/mission.

Cardinal, Rosalind. 2015. 6 Management Styles and When to Use Them. Article, *Huffington Post*. http://www.huffingtonpost. com/rosalind-cardinal/6-management-styles-and-when-to-use- them_b_6446960.html.

Chand, Smriti. 2015. 8 Types of Organisational Structures: Their Advantages and Disadvantages. Article, Your Article Library. http://www.yourarticlelibrary.com/organization/8-types- of-organisational-structures-their-advantages-and-disadvan- tages/22143/.

Chatterjee, Camille. 2015. 5 Personality Tests Hiring Managers are Using that Could Make or Break Your Next Job Interview. Article, *Business Insider*. http://www.msn.com/en-nz/money/ careersandeducation/5-personality-tests-hiring-managers- are-using-that-could-make-or-break-your-next-job-interview/ ar-BBl1TRB#page=1.

Chung, Elizabeth. 2015. 5 Nonprofits That Make Clean Water A Global Reality. Blog, Classy. http://www.classy.org/ blog/5-nonprofits-make-clean-water-global-reality/.

Clifton, Jim. 2013. State of the American Workplace. Report, Gallup Organization. http://employeeengagement.com/wp- content/uploads/2013/06/Gallup-2013-State-of-the-American- Workplace-Report.pdf.

Copeland, Mary Kay. 2014. The Emerging Significance of Values Based Leadership: A Literature Review. Article, *International Journal of Leadership Studies*, 8, no. 2. http://www.regent. edu/acad/global/publications/ijls/new/vol8iss2/6-Copeland. pdf.

Dowden, Craig. 2013. Want to be Liked as a Leader? Stop Treating Others as You Would Want to be Treated. Article, *Financial Post*. http://business.financialpost.com/executive/c-suite/want-to-be-liked-as-a-leader-stop-treating-others-as-you-would-want-to-be-treated.

Drucker, Peter. No date. Website. http://www.brainyquote.com/quotes/quotes/p/peterdruck143104.html.

Ellsburg, Daniel. 1961. Risk, Ambiguity and the Savage Axioms. Article, *The Quarterly Journal of Economics*. 75, no. 4 (November): 643–669.

Epstein, Irwin. 2009. *Clinical Data-Mining: Integrating Practice and Research*. Oxford, UK: Oxford University Press.

Feigenbaum, Eric. 2016. Purpose of Organizational Structure. Article, *Houston Chronicle*. http://smallbusiness.chron.com/purpose-organizational-structure-3812.html.

FitSM. 2016. Part 0: Overview and Vocabulary. *Standards for lightweight IT service management.* Service Standards. http://fitsm.itemo.org/sites/default/files/FitSM-0_Overview_and_vocabulary.pdf.

Frankl, Viktor. 1959. *Man's Search for Meaning*. Boston, MA: Beacon Press.

Gartland, Michael. 2009. Christians Defy Law to Convert Muslims in Tsunami Aftermath. Article, International Reporting Project. https://internationalreportingproject.org/stories/view/christians-defy-law-to-convert-muslims-in-tsunami-aftermath.

Goucher, Candice; LeGuin, Charles; and Watson, Linda. 1998. Ideas and Power: Goddesses, God-Kings, and Sages. In *In the Balance: Themes in World History*. Boston, MA: McGraw-Hill. https://www.learner.org/courses/worldhistory/support/reading_5_2.pdf.

Griffin, Ricky W. and Moorhead, Gregory. 2014. *Organizational Behavior: Managing People and Organizations*. Mason, OH: South-Western.

Harper, Douglas. 2016. Definition of Manage. Entry, Online Etymology Dictionary. http://www.etymonline.com/index.php?term=manage.

Hassell, David. 2013. Employees Quit Leaders, Not Companies. Article, *Talent Culture*. http://www.talentculture.com/employees-quit-leaders-companies/.

Hayden, Jeff. 2014. Top 50 Leadership and Management Experts. Article, *Inc*. http://www.inc.com/jeff-haden/the-top-50-leadership-and-management-experts-mon.html.

Haynes, Marina and Moore-Crawford, Cassandra. 1996. ANSC 455 Animal Behavior Laboratory Exercise 7 Social Dominance. Handout. http://terpconnect.umd.edu/~wrstrick/secu/ansc455/lab7.htm.

Ikram, Salima. 2006. The Afterlife in Ancient Egypt. Interview, *Nova*. http://www.pbs.org/wgbh/nova/ancient/afterlife-ancient-egypt.html.

Independent Sector. 2016. Checklist for Developing a Statement of Values and Code of Ethics. Webpage. http://independentsector.org/resource/checklist-code-ethics/.

Inglehart, Robert and Welzel, Christian. 2005. *Modernization, Cultural Change, and Democracy: The Human Development Sequence*. New York: Cambridge University Press.

Ingram, David. 2016. Why Is Organizational Structure Important? Article, *Houston Chronicle*. http://smallbusiness.chron.com/organizational-structure-important-3793.html.

International Rescue Committee. 2016a. Mission Statement. http://www.rescue.org/history.

International Rescue Committee. 2016b. Values Statement. http://www.rescue.org/values-irc-0.

Jacobides, Michael G. 2007. The Inherent Limits of Organizational Structure and the Unfulfilled Role of Hierarchy: Lessons from a Near-War. *Organization Science*, 18, no. 3: 455–477.

Johnson, Gary T. and Lewis, Russell L. 2010. *Lessons Learned about Nonprofit Management and Finance*. Chicago, IL: Chicago Historical Society, p. 95.

Kanter, Rosabeth Moss. 2013. Three Things that Actually Motivate Employees. Article, *Harvard Business Review*. https://hbr.org/2013/10/three-things-that-actually-motivate-employees.

Kastner, Alton. No date. A Brief History of the International Rescue Committee. Article, International Rescue Committee. https://www.rescue-uk.org/sites/default/files/document/999/abriefhistoryoftheirc0.pdf.

Kempster, Norman. 1998. Searching for a Stable Peace in Bosnia, Kosovo and Cyprus: Interview with Richard Holbrooke. Article, *Los Angeles Times*. http://articles.latimes.com/1998/jun/07/opinion/op-57627.

Kramer, Harry M. 2011. *From Values to Action: The Four Principles of Values-based Leadership*. San Francisco, CA: Jossey Bass.

Lipman, Victor. 2015a. People Leave Managers, Not Companies. Article, *Forbes*. http://www.forbes.com/sites/victorlipman/2015/08/04/people-leave-managers-not-companies/#468610ac16f3.

Lipman, Victor. 2015b. *The Type B Manager: Leading Successfully in a Type A World*. New York: Prentice Hall.

Lund, Jeb. 2014. The 15 Worst Owners in Sports. Article, *Rolling Stone*. http://www.rollingstone.com/culture/lists/the-15-worst-owners-in-sports-20141125/mike-brown-cincinnati-bengals-20141125.

Manuel, Paul Christopher; Reardon, Lawrence C.; and Wilcox, Clyde. Eds. 2006. *The Catholic Church and the Nation-State, Comparative Perspectives*. Washington, DC: Georgetown University Press.

Meinert, Dori. 2015. What Do Personality Tests Really Reveal? Article, Society for Human Resource Management. https://www.shrm.org/hr-today/news/hr-magazine/pages/0615-personality-tests.aspx.

Merriam-Webster. 2016. Definition of Mission. Entry. http://www.merriam-webster.com/dictionary/mission.

Mill, John Stuart. *On Liberty*. London: Longman, Roberts & Green, 1869; Bartleby.com, 1999. www.bartleby.com/130/

Morgan, Jacob. 2014. *The Future of Work: Attract New Talent, Build Better Leaders, and Create a Competitive Organization*. Wiley, NJ: Wiley.

Morgeson, Frederick P. and Humphrey, Stephen E. 2006. The Work Design Questionnaire (WDQ): Developing and Validating a Comprehensive Measure for Assessing Job Design and the Nature of Work. Article, *Journal of Applied Psychology*, 91, no. 6 (November): 1321–1339. http://dx.doi.org/10.1037/0021-9010.91.6.1321.

National Susan B. Anthony Museum and House. 2013. Biography of Susan B. Anthony. Article. http://susanbanthonyhouse.org/her-story/biography.php.

Native Languages of the Americas. 2015. Native American Legends: Sky Woman (Ataensic, Atahensic, Ataentsic). Article. http://www.native-languages.org/morelegends/sky-woman.htm.

Nelson Mandela Foundation. 2016. FAQs. Webpage. https://www.nelsonmandela.org/content/page/faqs.

Oswald, Andrew J.; Pronto, Eugenio; and Sgroi, Daniel. 2014. Happiness and Productivity. Working Paper, University of Warwick, UK, and IZA Bonn, Germany. https://www2.warwick.ac.uk/fac/soc/economics/staff/eproto/workingpapers/happinessproductivity.pdf.

Oxfam. 2016. Statement of Beliefs. https://www.oxfam.org/en/our-purpose-and-beliefs.

Oxfam. 2017. *Stichting Oxfam International Code of Conduct.* https://www.oxfam.org/sites/www.oxfam.org/files/file_attachments/story/codeofconductoct11_1_0.pdf.

Oxford English Dictionary. 2016. https://en.oxforddictionaries.com.

Percival, David and Shelton, Robert D. 2013. Unleashing the Power of Innovation. Report, PriceWaterhouse Coopers.

Pippin, Robert B. 2005. *The Persistence of Subjectivity: On the Kantian Aftermath.* New York: Cambridge University Press.

Public Health Action Support Team. 2011. Understanding the Internal and External Organisational Environments: Evaluating Internal Resources and Organisational Capabilities. Article, HealthKnowledge. http://www.healthknowledge.org.uk/public-health-textbook/organisation-management/5b-understanding-ofs/internal-external.

Saxton, Gregory D. 2012. The Participatory Revolution in Nonprofit Management. Article, *Nonprofit Quarterly.* https://nonprofitquarterly.org/2012/08/02/the-participatory-revolution-in-nonprofit-management/?utm_source=Daily+Newswire&utm_campaign=eadb0b4af7-Daily_Digest_23497_14_2016&utm_medium=email&utm_term=0_94063a1d17-eadb0b4af7-12324385.

Saylor Foundation. 2013. Values-Based Leadership. Course document. https://www.saylor.org/site/wp-content/uploads/2013/09/Saylor.orgs-Values-Based-Leadership.pdf.

Schwartz, Shalom H. 2006. Basic Human Values: Theory, Methods, and Application. Article, *Revue française de sociologie,* 47, no. 4: 9.

Schwartz, Shalom. H.; Melech, Gila; Lehmann, Arielle; Burgess, Steven; Harris, Mari; and Owens, Vicki. 2001. Extending the Cross-Cultural Validity of the Theory of Basic Human Values with a Different Method of Measurement. Article, *Journal of Cross-Cultural Psychology,* 32, no. 5 (September): 519–542.

Snyder, Benjamin. 2015. Half of Us Have Quit Our Job Because of a Bad Boss. Article, *Fortune.* http://fortune.com/2015/04/02/quit-reasons/.

Splash. 2016. Mission Statement. Webpage. http://www.splash.org/.

The Thirst Project. 2016. Mission Statement. Webpage. https://www.thirstproject.org/.

Time. 2016. The 25 Most Influential Business Management Books. Article. http://content.time.com/time/specials/packages/completelist/0,29569,2086680,00.html.

Tolstoy, Leo Nikolayevich. 1900. Three Methods of Reform. Pamphlet. https://books.google.com/books?id=kVBYAAAAMA AJ&pg=PA71&lpg=PA71&dq=translation+of+tolstoy%27s+three+ methods+of+reform&source=bl&ots=epOjZOIw3x&sig=pClglg ajc8o2sxLGV1RWvTPtXuw&hl=en&sa=X&ved=0ahUKEwj_sea kkuPRAhVqyoMKHfbBAqAQ6AEIPjAI#v=onepage&q=tra nslation%20of%20tolstoy's%20three%20methods%20of%20 reform&f=false.

Tolstoy, Leo Nikolayevich. 1894. *The Kingdom of God is Within You*. New York: Wallachia Press.

Top Management Degrees. 2016. Top 50 Best Selling Management Books of All Time. Article. http://www.topmanagementdegrees. com/management-books/.

Top Nonprofits. 2016. Fifty Example Mission Statements. Article. https://topnonprofits.com/examples/ nonprofit-mission-statements/.

UNESCO. 2013. Girl's Education: The Facts. Education for All GMR Fact Sheet. http://en.unesco.org/gem-report/sites/gem-report/ files/girls-factsheet-en.pdf.

UNICEF. 2003. *The State of the World's Children*. New York: UNICEF.

Unitarian Universalist Association. 2016. What We Believe. Webpage. http://www.uua.org/beliefs/what-we-believe.

United Nations. 1945. Charter of the United Nations. Document. http://www.un.org/en/sections/un-charter/introductory-note/ index.html.

United Nations. 1948. Universal Declaration of Human Rights. Document. http://www.ohchr.org/EN/UDHR/Documents/ UDHR_Translations/eng.pdf.

United States Department of State. 2011. Country Reports on Human Rights Practices for 2011. Report, Bureau of Democracy, Human Rights and Labor. https://www. state.gov/j/drl/rls/hrrpt/2011humanrightsreport/index. htm?dynamic_load_id=186163#wrapper.

Vigeland, Tess. 2015. *Leap*. New York: Harmony.

Vocabulary.com. 2016. Definition of Mission. Entry. http://www. vocabulary.com/dictionary/mission.

Wall Street Journal. 2009. What is the Difference Between Management and Leadership? Article, adapted from *The Wall Street Journal Complete Small Business Guidebook*. http://guides.wsj.com/management/developing-a-leadership-style/what-is-the-difference-between-management-and-leadership/.

Watson, Tom. 2011. Consumer Philanthropy: Nonprofits Spend Billions to Reach Consumers. Article, *Huffington Post*. http://www.huffingtonpost.com/tom-watson/consumer-philanthropy-non_b_36261.html.

Webbert, David. 2014. Were Ben & Jerry Right About Ice Cream and Fair Pay? Article, *Portland Press Herald*. http://contributors.pressherald.com/business/on-the-job/ben-jerry-right-ice-cream-fair-pay/.

Whitfield, Bob. 2001. *The Extension of the Franchise*, 1832–1931. Oxford: Heinemann Educational Publishers.

Whitman, Walt. 2007. *Leaves of Grass*. Brooklyn, NY: Walt Whitman.

Zirin, David. (2010). *Bad Sports: How Owners are Ruining the Games We Love*. New York: Simon and Schuster.

Index

V

Vacation, 211–213
Values, and beliefs, 109–110
Values-Based Leadership (VBL), 65–66
Values Statement, 55, 71, 72, 75, 76, 80, 103
Value system, 55–78
VBL, *see* Values-Based Leadership (VBL)

W

Walking around, management by, 180–182, 235–236
Whitman, Walt, 52
Work behaviors, 237–238
World Values Survey, 60, 75, 132
Worth, 199–200

Z

Zirin, David, 173

Printed in the United States
by Baker & Taylor Publisher Services